NONE SO PRETTY

The Sexing of Rebecca Pine

None So Pretty

The Story of a Changing Life

Reg McKay

MAINSTREAM
PUBLISHING

EDINBURGH AND LONDON

First published in Great Britain in 1999 by
MAINSTREAM PUBLISHING COMPANY (EDINBURGH) LTD
7 Albany Street
Edinburgh EH1 3UG

ISBN 1 84018 175 3

A catalogue record for this book is available from the British Library

Typeset in Sabon
Printed and bound in Great Britain by Butler & Tanner Ltd

Contents

1 The Beginning of Wisdom

Ah, but a man's reach should exceed his grasp,
Or what's a heaven for?
ROBERT BROWNING IN 'ANDREA DEL SARTO'

The solitary man looked as if he would fall at any moment. Tall and slim, he bent into an invisible wind powerful up there, absent down here. The old-fashioned eyeglass discerned a grace as the man swayed with each swirl and blast. Moving with the force, the man ran the risk of being whisked in the direction of his interminable stare – out and in to the angry-edged sea loch. Or back and up over the long-legged stocking that is the peninsula. Down to the toe pointing a warning at Ireland then north to the scattered mess that is Islay, Jura, Iona and Mull. Newman wished the stranger the protection of such a Muse and free from a dread that may drop him on to the Loch Fyne-washed rocks below.

Newman's eyeglass had become frosted by the warm smir. Besides, it was growing heavy on her outstretched arm. The brass-bodied telescope looked good but was impractical for extended observation. Much like the story of her life, she thought. A snatch at this, a short run at that. She seemed to have done a little of much but not much of anything. Maybe she should have settled to her craft in a place like this, like Tarbert. A few hundred souls nestled on the isthmus of Kintyre. A fishing village where everyone was related to everyone. Where change was slow and life predictable. Where nothing different ever happened. Substance and seriousness was all. A village where you had to earn the respect of your neighbours over generations. A place where everybody knew exactly who they were.

Tarbert looked good in the November sun prevailing along with the drizzle. A classic sheltered semicircle of a harbour, framed by a sharp rise of rows of houses. The buildings' dark, mottled colours, sombre like the people. The hotels and pubs, bright beacons of azure, salmon pink and custard yellow. The hotels said, 'I'm here.' The homes said, 'I'm here to stay.'

A fishing boat chugged towards base, its heavy catch pilfered by swooping, squawking gulls. The sails of a yacht flapped and snapped as ruddy-faced enthusiasts steered her out for a late-afternoon adventure. An old, battered boat, of indeterminate function, muffled her engines as reverse gears pulled her back and slowed her down for a gentle thump, bump against the quay. Across the bay, two canoeists sparkled red and orange against the grey swell of waves, skirting the scattered rocks marking the far shore. 'As steady and predictable as the people,' Newman pondered. 'Why have I only just discovered this place?'

The glass dried, Newman turned her back on Tarbert and raised the telescope once again to the mannequin show on the cliff face above. The man had gone. Complementary flavours of interest and unease closed Newman's throat as she swept the promontory for human movement. Immediately she scanned the space between land and sea, the brown wet cliffs. If he had fallen it would have been on the blind side. Then a sweep of the land from the tip of the precipice, past the precariously perched houses, to the crusty walls of the castle ruins. The telescope was cursed as a limited tool with a scope of vision too narrow for the task. Then down the hill, searching for some pathway through the whins and the heather.

There he was, walking at a brisk pace downhill, closer than she imagined possible, swinging his arms and smiling. Newman watched as an erect, distinguished man moved towards her in a rapid, curving descent of the hill. The aged, brass device worked well enough to pull the stranger close to her eye, allowing her to watch unwatched. So she had done many times before to others. Collecting their habits, their mannerisms, their dress. Inventing lives for them which she would later use in her stories without so much as an acknowledgement. 'Borrowing strangers' she called it. People she would not see again, turning up in her stories. They may read those stories but would fail to recognise their reflections due to the warping of her imagination. The only thing she was good at, in her opinion. Imagining people do extreme things in unlikely places, 'And not a bit of it true '

But she recognised this stranger. Not as consciousness stirs into life at the vague memory of someone who shared a bus stop one wet morning. But as a cousin played with as a child or a brief romance during teenage years, too many decades before. This person had been significant for her at some point. Then it came back.

~

'Robert John Pine
Born 4 November 1930
In Birmingham, The Midlands, England.
Died in Tarbert, Loch Fyne, Argyll
In the Year 2000 and something . . .'

Robert Pine was rehearsing his gravestone not through any morbidity but in celebration. He had been in Tarbert only a few hours yet knew this was where he would stay. He stood on the rocks known as the Crow's Nest breathing the air and giving his thanks.

Weeks before, he and Jean had agreed to change their lives. To leave behind big town life and move to a place of their choice rather than where some employer determined they should live. Deciding on Scotland was easy. Jean was from Edinburgh and her children had been born there. Robert had always thought of himself as Scottish, though born in England of English parents. He had simply felt Scottish from as young as he could remember. Taking every chance to be the tourist, as a young man he had travelled with an older, car-owning friend all over Scotland. At least he had *thought* 'all over' until this morning, as he drove down the hill, past the trees and into the cruel beauty that is Tarbert.

Deciding on Scotland was easy. Deciding on east or west proved to be more problematic. He mourned how countries, counties, cities everywhere were split between north and south, east and west, town and burgh, inner and outer. This had never been his way. There was some good in everything and he always looked for the poetic, the fine curve and the colour. Or, at least, he left himself open and the beauty found him. There was some everywhere. Here the beauty abounded and overwhelmed.

Robert Pine knew what he liked and he preferred the warmth

and majesty of the West to the cold, fresh winds of the East. His view had prevailed and one night they had rummaged for a dog-eared map of Scotland.

'Where the pin strikes, we will live within a fifty-mile radius,' was the agreement. The nervous excitement was palpable and the pin struck Oban. He knew Oban and recollected the small, compact, ferry town. Small enough to feel belonging and big enough to support the diversity of their interests. A cultured town with traditions of music, the Mod, painting and writers. That night he had imagined himself in Oban and felt inspired.

The visit to Oban had been disappointing. It was still many of the things he had remembered but there was now an edge to it that spoke of money, profit, industry and in-fighting. Oban was neither one thing nor the other. With some relief he had realised that the property visited was beyond their means and they headed south towards the Mull of Kintyre.

The journey was one when everything seemed to go well. Three children in the back seat as the car wound round bends and back on itself, with rare respite. The potential for sickness, bad tempers and disinterest after days of traversing such routes was evident. He loved children, their naïvety, truthfulness and enthusiasm. In common with most adults, he suspected, childish whims, moans and fights irritated – but no such problem. He kept them amused with ancient tales of the wild boar of Kintyre being slain by Diarmid O'Duibhne to win his love from the vengeful Fingal; of Vikings and Magnus Bareleg wearing the kilt around Trondheim (dandy or punk? He preferred dandy, the children punk); how the same Magnus won Kintyre by having a boat dragged across the isthmus at Tarbert; the majesty of the boat with full sail and Magnus at the tiller. Of how Tarbert Castle was for years the only mainland refuge of Robert the Bruce as the English harried and worried after him. Of Campbells and MacDonalds and the massacre of Dunaverty being more brutal than that of Glencoe; of magic circles of standing stones and ancient wisdom which greeted Columba and waited for them now.

Tales of gore, romance and magic and only slightly embellished by the narrator with all the licence offered by the oral tradition. By the time they skirted the hill at Stonefield and descended into the village the children were convinced, expectant enthusiasts. 'But what they think now they've seen the village, now that is another question altogether,' was the only worry troubling Robert Pine as he moved in the blasts of warm, damp wind and gazed over the hills of Cowal and Bute to Arran beyond.

The solitary man was not about to fall. He had cherished hopes and plans. They would buy the cottage and the shop. Jean would run the bed and breakfast, he the shop. The former would help but the latter would be the dream. A haven to sell his art, to display his poetry. A hobby that was life. A means to a living demanding his creativity. A hobby no more, but life itself. His whole life.

The solitary man was experiencing a new beginning. No more would he hawk the wares of others around the mess that is Leeds or the chaos that is Birmingham. No more would he set out on the madness of motorways, racing against time. No more sales targets or conventions where the unconvinced would act convinced for a living. Robert Pine had been that someone else for years but no more. He would leave those parts of him behind in Harrogate and bring with him the light luggage of his essence. This would be his personal renaissance.

~

Jean was concerned about Robert. He had been so happy yet needed to go away on his own. They had arranged to meet at the Battery and the children were becoming fractious. She hoped he was not disappointed with Tarbert since she and all the children wanted to stay. Jackie, Kirsty and Campbell agreed unanimously – a rare event – they did not want to leave.

Then she saw him, winding his way down the hillside. Striding out briskly and obviously happy. He marched up to the group, his wife and her children, and asked in his charming, almost coquettish, manner, 'Well?'

Nearby, a middle-aged woman, dressed in the expensive, anorak uniform of the well-to-do visitor, rolled up a fine-looking brass telescope, tucked it under her arm and walked on by. As she passed the group, she sensed a celebration of agreement and the chatter of plans. She watched Sergeant Bob Pine embrace a handsome, younger woman and being surrounded by three tugging, smiling children. As she passed the huddle, she caught Bob Pine's eye and held it until she would have to have walked backwards to continue. A familiar quizzical look framed the face of her old colleague but no sense of recognition flickered, not even for an instant.

Newman walked on, knowing that Bob Pine would have forgotten the incident by the time she had reached her car. She wondered at the unchanging permanence of people. They lost hair, gained wrinkles, earned money and lost it. They had children and gave up their enthusiasms. Through it all they remained themselves, 'Still the same old Bob. Looking forward and never looking back.'

2 Suffer the Little Children

By education most have been misled;
So they believe, because they so were bred.
The priest continues what the nurse began,
And thus the child imposes on the man.
JOHN DRYDEN IN 'THE HIND AND THE PANTHER'

Oldbury, Midlands, England. 1937.
The seven-year-old boy stood at his bedroom window and stared out at the empty street.

It was a hot July day and he loved the feeling of warmth and freedom. Wearing light shorts and his favourite shirt, matching ankle socks neatly folded, just as Mother had taught him. The final symbol was permission, requirement even, to wear his sandals, all brown leather and heavy side buckles. This was surely summer and holidays. Time for play.

On the way, he had skipped and hopped, avoiding the lines and escaping the bears.

Reaching the gate he stretched up and pushed the metal latch free. He had to be careful passing through the front garden where children were not allowed. Watching his toes take every step, he followed the path around the side to the yard at the back. As he passed the gable end, the girls' chatter swelled and increased into voices and an involuntary skip escaped his guarded toes.

Robert was too innocent to notice the looks of exasperation passing between the girls. Instead he heard only the words that they would play hide and seek and he was first. Leaning against the shed door, arms covering his head, eyes clamped shut, he counted slowly and deliberately. Robert Pine played fair just as Father had taught. 'Here I come, ready or not!' and off he searched in all the usual places. Searched and searched and searched. Then he looked in the most unusual places. Along the street to the edge of parental limits and hovered there looking up and down the busier thoroughfare. The girls should not have gone that far. It was against the rules.

The girls were gone. They did not want Robert with them. The girls were not playing this game and not with him, the boy. Robert wandered home, dragging his sandals on the pavement, using his toes to slow him down. The child's despair increased, realising the scolding he would get from Mother that night for the scuff marks on his footwear. Homewards to his room where he would soon forget the girls, for the moment.

Robert usually played with his sister, Bettina, and her friends. Played with them all, joining in all of their games. The best times were when they could be all together, like now in summer or weekends. They would play skipping rope and queue up in long lines, jumping in on turn and the verse of the rhyme would change, sing-songing on for ever, it seemed; or houses when they made believe they were a family each with his or her part. The themes would go on all day and sometimes the next. This was one of his favourite games and he did not mind much who his character was – mother, father, daughter, son, shopkeeper, neighbour. While the others bickered he would set about the props and the outfits. Laying out the empty Ovaltine tins, Persil packets, tobacco tins, jam jars and the chipped cups, he busied himself till the others settled and the game began.

Rain and confinement indoors did not bother him at all. Then they would read, dress up in the oversized clothes of dead relatives and, when allowed, listen to the wireless. As the youngest, Robert felt privileged to be part of the group. In summer he'd wake up with a buzz of anticipation, whirl through his ablutions, gulp down breakfast and go looking for his friends, the girls. As he had that morning, only to be excluded.

Alone in his room he quickly forgot the slight. Robert forgave the girls most things. When they giggled and whispered to each other he did not mind or make a fuss. He giggled and whispered too, though he did not have their secret and they would not share it. Robert admired the girls.

Opening the drawer, Robert touched his sister's clothes. He drew his hand across white and grey socks, over folded, white underwear and on to the blouses decorated with raised flowers at the borders. Leaving the drawer open, he crossed to the large, shiny wardrobe, the one shared with Bettina. Standing on tiptoe and twisting at the key, it hurt his hand, as always, leaving angry red ridges on his thumb and fingers. Using two hands was easier, but still hurt. Mother would lean a shoulder against the door and unlock it with a quick, crisp click – one-handed as her other arm cradled the freshly ironed clothes, still smelling warm and welcoming.

Clunk. The wardrobe door sprung open as he leaned over and rubbed his hands together between his legs. Blowing on hot fingers as he had seen workmen do as they bent to lift picks and shovels and excavate deep, mysterious holes in the road, he approached the clothes hanging in an orderly queue. To the left, his Sunday best. To the right, his sister's finery and dresses too long to fold into drawers. Stepping into the darkened cell he felt its dark, musty atmosphere engulf and comfort him. Reaching up, he pulled a dress and hanger down and held it to his body.

Leaving the bedroom, he turned and checked, 'Drawer closed. Wardrobe shut and locked.' All was as it had been. The secret was important though Robert did not know why.

~

Herefordshire, England. 1938.
The Pine family was doing well. Father's job as Personal Assistant to the Director of Birmingham and Midlands Omnibus Co. and Mother's in the Tax Office were steady, clean and well paid. Robert, the child, had a sense of this as he met other children at school who did not have as much as the Pines.

Some children always wore the same clothes or the same pair of boots whatever the weather. He envied the boots as they crunched and sparked on the road, more iron than leather in the soles. The boys had no Sunday best, the girls no party frocks. In summer they looked as drab and muffled as they did in winter. Even then, Robert sensed he did not want to be without and to live a life that was impoverished. No more than a sense since he was still engrossed in that self-centredness that is childhood when every boy believes he is a prince, every girl a princess. He knew what he wanted and in summer that included a holiday. Even some people who lived on his street could not afford a holiday. Some of them pretended they could by sending their children away to an aunt or uncle while the adults continued life at home and at work as usual.

The Pines were going on a real holiday. A farm in

Herefordshire for two weeks, the whole family. This was an event for all of them and preparation started weeks before. Cases were dragged down from the loft and wiped free of dust. Summer clothes, swimming trunks and special purchases were to be packed away in good time. Mother believed in preparation and planning ahead. Last-minute scramblings were 'an unnecessary hindrance, irritating and avoidable'. All were to play their part and did so willingly with care, precision and anticipation.

Young Robert made some special preparations. He wanted to be sure he had everything he needed. These were special items and not simply a matter of working through the lists written in Father's fine script. Choosing the items was easy and he wrapped them individually, alone in his room. Sheets from the newspaper pile, stored for fire lighting and unlikely to be missed, made the parcels anonymous. Each little bundle was folded, covered and placed in the case. A task well done. Mother would approve.

The day of departure passed smoothly and they set off on bicycles happy, relaxed, released. Mother, as ever, had been right. Herefordshire was all he had hoped. But his special little newspaper-shrouded packages were not there in the case where he had placed them. Someone had not trusted the packing and checked. All his surprises had been removed.

Bettina did not mention the purloining of her underwear. Mother said nothing. Father said nothing. Robert said nothing. He enjoyed the holiday.

~

Oldbury, Midlands, England. 1939.
Bedtime was strictly adhered to in the Pine house. By 8 o'clock each night, both Bettina and Robert were washed, fed and snug in the thick, heavy blankets of their bed. Striped cotton pyjamas were a signal that the day had come to a close, save for brushing teeth, prayers and a short while reading. The house took on a hushed, reverential tone peculiar to the business of bedding down. Mother and Father would sit in the front room quietly reading, talking or listening to the wireless. No noise or disturbance was allowed after that hour.

Father would write his works' magazine, draw or read. Sometimes he would make additions to his scrapbooks.

Carefully, he snipped around the magazine articles – sometimes cutting square, sometimes curving around the heads of the people, the steam engine or aeroplane in the picture. Working on the table, he flattened the thick, dark pages of his book and laid out the cuttings in a proposed montage. Satisfied with his composition, he tested the bottle of glue on a piece of waste paper, shaking the bottle and pushing down firmly on the amber rubber, ensuring a smooth and even flow. As he pressed delicately on the damp additions with a folded cloth, the scraps did not buckle or blister.

Mother would sit by the fire sewing or knitting. More often she would read or chat to Father. Sometimes she would speak of politics, the Conservative Party and the war. She would do something, she would help but not quite yet. The wireless murmured in the background. Evenings were a hallowed time broken only by sickness, civil commotion or disaster.

The cotton-lined cocoon that is a child's shape in bed was warmed and ready for the night's comfort when Robert was called downstairs. Traipsing down the dull stairwell, he stopped to pull up his slipping cotton trousers high at the waist. Holding the cord with one hand he walked firmly and deliberately, one stair at a time, careful not to trip. The sitting room was bright and warm from the coal fire. The blackout blinds were drawn and created a feeling of being shut in, safe and sound. Sitting and waiting for some special purpose, the two adults dominated the room. As he stood on the linoleum before them, tugging his trousers up, he smiled and waited for the warmth expected from his parents.

He could not recall what he had done. Whatever it was he must have been bad. Both parents spoke but it was Father's question which hung in the air: 'You don't want to be a girl now do you, Bob?'

Standing on the cold floor, rubbing the sole of one naked foot on the arch of the other, Robert's brow felt fevered and fingers light and useless as they fidgeted with the thick, cotton cuffs falling short of his thin wrists. The child's gaze stared down at somewhere in the pattern of the fireside rug, seeing nothing. His lips were dry and would not move. Little Robert stood fixed to the spot by a question he did not understand from parents he loved. What had he done? What was so bad to deserve this audience? What did the question mean? What answer did they want? Yes or no? Yes or no? Fixed for ever it seemed till he gasped a lung full of air, drew his chin to his chest and squeaked, 'No.'

The answer was rewarded immediately by Mother. 'Of course you don't, Robert. That's a good boy. Now off to bed with you and no more of this nonsense.'

What nonsense? Little Robert Pine lay in bed that night relieved but worried. The boy did not know what he had done, did not understand the question nor his answer. The child felt he had cheated and let his parents down but did not know how.

Little Robert Pine lay in bed that night and cried himself to sleep.

3 The Promiscuous Witch
and the Spy

The rarer action is
In virtue than in vengeance.
SHAKESPEARE IN 'THE TEMPEST'

The road to Campbeltown was a cruel and tempting death trap. Leastwise that was Newman's first impression. A confident, easy-going city driver, she struggled and stuttered on the tarred zigzags of ancient routes which served as main roads. The roadwork-pocked stuttering yet watery seductiveness of Loch Lomond, up and over the Rest And Be Thankful, grinding and twisting through mid-Argyll. Reaching the road from Lochgilphead to Tarbert she thought she was on the final leg and an easy, rolling ride till she found herself again wedged between cliffs and loch side. Great clumps of grey rock looking both solid and fragile pushing the traffic out to the edge of a short drop to Loch Fyne. The loch's glitter drew tired, bored eyes and cars swerved momentarily across white lines as bend followed bend. All of this was a challenge she met hunched over the steering wheel, knuckles white with the tension of her grip, as carefree, rusting Escorts and Fiestas sped past her, driving blind on suicide bends. The road to Campbeltown seemed to be an end to all of that as it left Tarbert, stretching straight and wide. Newman opened her shoulder blades as she opened her accelerator. Soon, of course, the unexpected appeared.

West Loch was a short drive down the Campbeltown road and Newman promised herself she would not go the whole way too often – just when unavoidable. That was the only reason to go to Campbeltown, or so the locals advised. The Cottage was perfect. Hidden in the trees, hundreds of yards from the main thoroughfare and within sight of the Loch. She had a sense that she could see the Loch but the Loch could not see her. From her bedroom she watched the Islay ferry push into deeper water and thrash out away from the shore towards open seas. All purposeful energy on departure, on return it seemed wasted, exhausted, somnambulant.

The Loch and the Islands were Newman's privacy. Behind was Tarbert, human contact and life. In less than five minutes she could drive across the peninsula from west to east. In that time, she could leave behind solitude and dip into the relationships, gossip and business describing the people who made up the village. Just as quickly she could leave society and return to the waiting refuge, the Cottage.

Maybe here she could let go? Lately she had yearned for inclusion and the easy-going intimacy of neighbours. She would visit the Cottage often and be around the village a great deal. She would not bring carloads of provisions up from the city but would buy her food, cigarettes and newspapers here. She would mingle and nod 'hello', declaring herself safe to all around. She would join in the community life, the clubs, and taste the spirit of this place. Newman expected that the people made their own entertainment and looked forward to ceilidhs, country dancing, concerts, whist drives and fund raisers. Normality, ordinariness and certainty – Tarbert would provide her with an ample dosage of these medicines she craved.

First, the Cottage had to be brought up to her standards. One of those little, florid scars marking country rather than city was how people left the houses sold on to others. In the city, they were leaving more and more in the house – curtains, cookers, carpets, lampshades. You could move in your furniture and settle. Here they removed everything, stripped the place bare, unscrewed the unscrewable, leaving four walls and a roof. You were required to turn the house into a home by yourself and expect no help. Unless, of course, you paid more money. They had even removed the few fitted carpets. The rooms were sketched by internal walls travelling at crazed angles. Though many looked similar, these cottages were internally unique. She imagined the vendors searching for a new home where the floor plan matched the creative whims of the plasterers, joiners and stonemasons one hundred and fifty years ago. She also imagined the carpets rolled up and discarded on a sodden pavement, waiting for the refuse lorry.

Newman surveyed her new retreat and checked the list of

work to be done – carpets, joinery, a shower, plumbing, wood-burning stove. For these changes she needed the expertise of others. Painting, decorating and curtains, the dressing up, she would manage herself and would enjoy. The house would be transformed and improved in a month but would stay the same quaint Cottage. 'Much like people,' she thought.

~

Newman drew her car to a halt neatly between the lines marking the parking space. A row of white-edged slots bordered the lip of the harbour. Over the nose of the car was a sea view and a wave of vertigo momentarily dizzied Newman. Stepping from the vehicle, for an instant she anticipated falling down and down into deep, salty water, forever floating at the mercy of the tides. Feet safely on firm ground, she reached up, stretched her arms and twisted her back in the action of someone stiff from hours of driving. Newman had driven for minutes but needed the reassurance of the solidity and certainty of her body as an antidote to the fluidity of the Loch and expanse of the sky.

The light in Tarbert seemed crisp and sharp and she found herself wearing sunglasses even in cloudy weather. She appreciated the additional privacy of the dark glass and privately acknowledged her quest for a valid reason to take cover. Her imagination had witnessed her driving an open-topped Cadillac in downtown LA while homeboys languished in the lazy sun and gum-chewing, gun-carrying cops patrolled the streets, ignoring the long-haired, bare-legged women touting for business on hot sidewalks. There she would wear shades and feel at ease. Here, in archaic Argyll, she felt comfort in protection from the low-slung November sun peering over the craggy, eroded volcanoes and fir-strewn tracks left by glaciers in another time. What the sun lacked in warmth it made up for in annoyance.

Remembering to remove her sunglasses, Newman entered the hotel lounge bar and was clouded by billows of cigarette smoke, the drone of conversation and the under-tang of bitter-smelling beer. A coal fire, licking the hearth, should have been the focal point but was ignored by most of the men as they went about their social business. The accents were local and still felt foreign to her ears. These pubs reminded her of travels as a youth, hitch-hiking across Spain and France when a limited budget called for the use of the cheaper local facilities. The only difference was the smell of the tobacco, though the pipe smoker in the corner added an exotic, scented flavour to the dull, acrid aroma of British cigarettes.

The visit combined business and pleasure. Newman would have lunch and a drink but would engage the barman to carry out some work on the Cottage. The man had a reputation of loving wood and being capable of fine work. Wood was his pastime, his pleasure, his life's occupation while serving drinks paid the bills. When offered the work at the Cottage he responded with quiet, polite ambivalence. Newman had assumed some positive response at the prospect of extra income but was left wondering if he was interested in the work and doubted he would turn up at the appointed time to assess and price the job. His initial response was to 'pop round some time next week' and only an explanation that she would be in the area for a few days levered him in to a more immediate offer. As they agreed the arrangement, Newman thought she detected a hint of resentment.

The barman was only slightly more comfortable with an order for lunch. Taking a note of the food with silent nods he left the room without comment. Newman decided the order had been taken and a meal would appear in due course. Carrying her drink, she carefully negotiated the mess of tables and drinkers and found a place in a far corner by a window. From here she could watch everybody and eavesdrop every conversation without being observed, another old habit. She mentally castigated herself for falling into old, unsociable ways and promised she would change soon, soon but not quite yet.

At the next table a group of men were animated and loud in discussion. Three of the group held light-hearted postures while one adopted a serious and concerned demeanour. The topic was Hallowe'en night past. In Tarbert, apparently, adults as well as children would dress up to celebrate that night. Some years there would be a dance where everyone was expected to attend and in costume. The village made a good job of keeping the witches at bay. Newman had already noted the profusion of rowan trees, an ancient panoply of charms against evil spells, warlocks, witches and the dead. She wondered if the villagers had been grouping together for centuries in an effort to ward off the spirits, and how successful they had been.

On Hallowe'en night past, there had been the usual majority

of children dressed in ghost sheets, elaborate home-made witches' cloaks, cowboy costumes or mixed up combinations of items whose meaning had been lost as soon as they left home. The lunchtime drinkers agreed that Hallowe'en was a night for the children. There had been adults whose star-and-crescent-moon-spangled wraps and pointed hats had obviously been hired; grown women in elaborate rubber masks complete with curving pointed chins, warts and hairy moles; and at least two Frankenstein's monsters had turned up. A tall figure, resplendent in rubber pig mask, fedora and dirty trench coat swigged vodka and coke from a pint glass and flirted outrageously with everyone; a drunk warlock had tried to fly off a table on a borrowed broomstick. Some adult told the children that a particularly grotesque bogeyman was not dressed up at all, did not come from Tarbert but lived in a reclusive bothy high up on the hills, coming down only on Hallowe'en night. The bogeyman obliged by speaking in tongues and running after screaming, near-hysterical youngsters at every opportunity. His performance, helped by his intake of whisky, ended abruptly when he suddenly pulled his mask off to vomit at the feet of the accordionist, mid-reel. A certain rubber-masked witch had been discovered being too intimate with a heavy-booted monster, betrothed to another witch entirely. Mostly, Hallowe'en night in Tarbert had gone according to form.

The talk of the village was not the usual drunken shenanigans but the costume of one villager in particular. A man had turned up dressed as a woman. Not as a shapeless hag of a witch or as a clumsy, well-padded pantomime ugly sister but in a short, frilly dress, with stockings, make-up and shoes with heels. An immaculate and sexual bunny girl-type costume, matching his wife's outfit. Three of the men were laughing and talking of Danny La Rue. The serious one persisted. He was interrupted by suggestions of jealousy, his wife being rather plain. Still he persisted, to be told to cool down, that it had been a laugh and nothing more. When he shared the rumour that the man had made the costume himself, the group hooted with laughter and he was reminded that 'men are the best kilt makers'. But still he argued on till instructed it was his turn to buy the drinks.

Newman had to get back to the Cottage to meet a plumber. As she reached the door she caught the protester's next comment, shouted to his colleagues across the crowded room,

'It's Kiltie's children I feel sorry for. They're only wee and what a ribbing they're getting at school . . .'

~

Her mind still full of the stolen conversation, Newman stopped at the newsagents on the way back to her car. Buying that day's papers she explained she would be at the Cottage some weekends and asked how to obtain all the national Sunday papers. The shopkeeper shook her head and explained with a smile that only one shop sold Sunday papers, 'You'll want Kiltie's up the road. Ye canna miss him – tall man in a kilt. Bob Pine.'

4 Pert as a
Schoolgirl at War

Has he luck?
NAPOLEON BONAPARTE

King Edward's School, Birmingham, England. 1943.
The school was a minor public school: Mother would not have settled for anything less, with her standards and expectations. Bettina and Robert were constantly reminded of the importance of education in giving the best start to life and were intuitively aware of their parents' sacrifices to buy them the best they could afford. How childhood is the 'happiest time of your life' and how Mother would have been a teacher but 'things were different then. Women were expected to get married and raise a family. Now, anything is possible. Yes, there is no finer profession than teaching. You only get one chance.' Robert was enjoying school, managing to avoid taking anything too seriously.

Sitting in the classroom, he listened to the teacher with one ear and with both eyes watched the girls doing Physical Education outside. They stood in rows and performed synchronised physical jerks interspersed by softer, sweeping motions like an Isadora Duncan dance. Unlike Isadora's Fairies, these schoolgirls wore thickset green dresses, knee-length socks and blouses fastened high at the neck. Their growing, womanly shapes confounded the uniforms and the moral intentions of the school governors. Next to Robert sat another boy whispering his appreciation of the show and demonstrating what he liked about the humps and bumps of the straining girls. Pulling at the front of his blazer with both hands, he formed sharp, pointed, pubescent breast shapes and licked his lips with lascivious candour.

Rolling up two jotters, Robert slipped them into the front of his white shirt. Adjustments to the exercise books produced a more solid, though angular, bosom. His companion in crime giggled and nudged the boy next to him. Someone snorted too loudly and the teacher turned from his chalk scratchings on the board to catch Robert showing off his new chest profile. 'Boy! What are you playing at? Come here this instant!' he bellowed. 'No! No! Leave your shirt be. Come and show the class. Now!'

The walk to the front, between rows of desks of grinning teenage boys did not worry Robert Pine – in fact, he considered it a coup. Sexual innuendo was the currency of that age. His actions were neither dire nor serious so the punishment, if any, was likely to be minor. Besides, Robert Pine was artistic, did not enjoy mathematics and had no ambitions in that field. As he walked centre stage he played to the audience.

The teacher's black gown smelled of chalk, disinfectant and stale tobacco. When he spoke, he shouted and sprayed the boy's face with spittle. His breath stank, meaty and bitter. 'Stand up straight and face the class, Pine. Stop that sniggering now.'

From the front, the class seemed bigger and the number of boys endless. The male faces were either twitching with barely controlled glee or still, stoic grimaces refusing to respond to the humour. Robert recognised this latter trait as a posture to be adopted in disassociating oneself from the trouble and the culprit. It was common for teachers to punish not just the guilty but those who failed to stop the wrong-doing. Whole classes would be punished for the acts of one boy. Punishment sometimes involved whipping with a cane.

'Well, Pine. Stand up straight and let us see you. What have you got to say for yourself, lad? Just look at you. You are a disgrace,' shouted the teacher pointing at the sharp, conical breasts. 'You really want to be down there, don't you? Doing ladylike stretches with the girls.' The teacher smiled at the class, authorising mockery of the accused. All laughed. 'We could arrange for you to enter school via the Girls' gate in future.' The most frightened children laughed loudest. 'Maybe your mother could get you a little green pinafore, hmm?' Hysteria broke out in the ranks. The master was in a good mood. 'All right, that's enough! That's enough! Quiet! You don't want to be sent down to join in with the girls, do you really, Pine?'

'No, Sir.'

'Right. Well, sort yourself, lad. Now get back to your seat and pay attention.'

As Robert walked back up the aisle, dismantling the troublesome prostheses, here and there a boy winked or smiled, showing solidarity and gratitude for the diversion.

~

Oldbury, Midlands, England. 1943.

The children treated the war like a game, exciting but not a matter of life and death. All sorts of changes had occurred and week to week they did not know what to expect next. 'Careless talk costs lives' went the slogan. So troops would rumble by on roaring, camouflaged trucks with dull, painted headlamps looking ghostly in the half-light of the moon. Those bystanders wondering out loud where the convoy may be headed were castigated by neighbours and accused of disloyal behaviour, the ultimate sin. Some nights the droning beat of German aircraft could be heard crossing above the house, targeting the production lines of Coventry. From their shelter, the imaginations of young, fertile minds could chart the progress of battle, starting with the cack-cack-cack of the anti-aircraft guns and shells exploding with hollow thumps high above. Yellow and blue illuminations painted the sky, broken only by the red, dotted streaks of artillery fire, blindly seeking out the attacking planes. Sometimes it would end there, fizzling out in the realisation of the pursuit of spectres, the disappointment of the children being matched by the relief of the Air Defence crews. Other nights, louder bangs were followed by balls of red, orange and blue bursting in the sky then spiralling downwards in balls of yellow flame with comet tails, heralding a direct hit and cheered by the onlookers perched in their suburban sanctuary.

The children spared no thought for the people in the factories, hiding under their workbenches as masonry and beams were blasted loose and sent down to smash into machines, vehicles and scurrying bodies. No consideration was given to those city dwellers called by sirens from their air raid shelters to find their homes reduced to debris, everything gone. Of little serious merit was the plight of children taken from their parents and evacuated to havens in the country, safe from bombs but vulnerable to other perils the least of which was loneliness. As for that pilot, that German pilot, trapped in his seat in a craft of flames hurtling towards earth and his death – well they positively cheered his fate. 'One up for Tommy!'

'Serve you right, Hans!'

'Burn, Rabbit, burn!'

The children were not cruel, it was just that the war seemed unreal to them. They were close enough to witness and distant enough to be safe. Nobody really died, nobody they knew.

Even when Father got dressed up in his Air Warden's uniform and went out late at night to check the curfew and the blackout, they thought it a laugh. He was not at any risk, was he? The question did not occur to the children.

At the cinema they watched Pathé newsreels on the Allied invasion of Italy and cheered every heroic and partisan comment from the narrator. They shouted and cheered as armoured tanks moved through Mediterranean villages and soldiers fired long rifles at shuttered windows. They booed and hissed when Italian prisoners, arms aloft, were frog-marched out of bruised and broken houses. The narrator's observation that many Italian soldiers were mere children, malnourished and frightened, went unheard as the crescendo of vicious howls, thumped feet and rat-a-tat-tat of simulated machine guns filled the emporium from the raucous home supporters in the front rows. The admonitory comments from adults present were half-hearted and mild. Some grown-ups joined in and on the rare news of an Allied victory, spontaneously broke into a chorus of 'Rule Britannia'. Usherettes, usually fierce and uncompromising in the demonstration of their control and upholding a silent order, smiled and allowed the uproar for the duration. The rectitude of youth was admirable and had to be supported, 'There is a war on, you know.'

Pathé News was little more than a warm-up to the main film for the children. A *Hopalong Cassidy* or *Zorro* of a series, except real. A prelude to *Northwest Passage*, *The Great Dictator* or *Spitfire*. Good fun but not real, certainly not real.

One day, soldiers came and started work in the field at the end of their street. Lorries, jeeps and other traffic busied about all day and the children watched from the edge of the field, the closest they were allowed. Curiosity grew to excitement when the purpose of the labours was revealed as the raising of a barrage balloon. At the end of their street where there was no factory, munitions dump or army barracks, just their homes. The children thought that they must be important to be protected that way until disabused by an older boy. He explained that Oldbury was at the edge of the Black Country and on the direct route, east to west, for the enemy bombers. If the aeroplanes could not fly this way, the factories were safer. Simple, straightforward and disappointing. The children got used to the barrage balloon in time and almost forgot it was there.

One night, the air raid warning sounded with wailing sirens, rousing the Pines from their beds and sending them rushing to the Anderson shelter at the bottom of the garden. The event was not unusual and had passed without incident on many occasions. The shelter's brick walls and corrugated iron roof did not keep out the cold or the noise of low-flying aircraft. That night there was obviously sky-raised traffic of interest. The noise of war visited them that night and would be retold by the children in terms of 'crash, bang and wallop', terms too light to reflect their fear and panic.

Emerging from the shelter, many hours later, the Pines were told that the Germans had changed their tactics. Rather than bombs, they were dropping mines by parachute. Such a device had strayed off course and hit Oldbury. The mine had floated over a petrol station and landed in a field adjoining their home. A field full of soft, brown earth. The explosion transformed fertile mud into lethal projectiles soaring high into the air and onto the houses nearby. The Pines picked their way through their garden, now dented by huge lumps of stony, spiked turf, and looked at their home, smeared and sullied by excrement-coloured goo and dubs. War had visited them in an unexpected way.

Checking the inside of their home, they found broken windows and minor damage. Still they felt that they had been violated and burgled by a careless thief, more intent on leaving his mark and depositing his faeces than on stealing valuables. Wandering through the house and up the stairs, they checked the bedrooms one by one.

In one room, a slab of mud had hurtled through the roof, scoring a perfect hit on a bed. The bed's back was broken, the head and foot tilting inwards in the obtuse angles of splintered, useless limbs. The Pines stared at the bed feeling a sense of horror and violence. In the manner of funerals and hospital visits, Mother stated the obvious in an effort to exorcise thoughts of what could have happened that night and might happen soon, 'Oh, Robert, your bed. What a mess.'

~

King Edward's School, Birmingham, England. 1944.

The entrance to the school looked more grand on the way in than on the way out. Now his developing artist's eye understood the impact of lines, angles and objects but on his first day Robert had puzzled over this phenomenon and wanted to know if everyone saw the avenue this way but were reluctant to say. He had learned quickly what was and was not allowed among the boys, almost as quickly as he had learned the formal rules of the masters. Since that first year he had also learned numerous ways to cheat on the school rules without being caught, such behaviour being almost obligatory. Cheating on the unspoken regulations of his peers was a far riskier enterprise entirely.

He had parked his cycle at his usual place that morning and gone back and waited for his girlfriend to arrive off her tram. He really did not like mornings and as usual had been running late. Time could be shaved off the journey to school, depending how fast he rode the bike, and that morning he had gone flat out. As he cut across the main junction, he did not realise he was being more careless than usual. It was important to meet your girl and walk her up the avenue along with other couples. Your girl would be embarrassed if you failed to show and there would be talk. Besides Robert enjoyed these chats and strolls and they started the day just right.

The car had almost hit him and the driver had blasted his horn even while swerving with the pull of the brakes. Robert had been a little shaken after the event but had not stopped or hesitated, merely flushed hot as he sped away. The bike could really spin along when it had to, dropping a gear and tyres skidding as he rounded bends. Debonair is how he thought he looked and was glad Father had bought a Triumph with straight handle bars rather than a more stolid black Raleigh. When Father brought the bicycle home, having bought it second hand from a man in the next street, Robert had been grateful but secretly wished it had been a racer with curved handle bars, thin frame and complicated, dangling gear mechanisms. Boys with racers seemed somehow sleek, exotic and continental. He later changed his mind as he observed the riders bent over their steeds, backs bent and heads down. The whole business lacked dignity, an attribute he was beginning to recognise and value.

Walking with your girlfriend up to the school boundary was one of the rare opportunities for boys and girls to be together. At all times during the curriculum, any contact the boys had with the opposite sex was strictly limited to female staff and there were few of those. There were really two schools, a boys' and a girls' school. Different classrooms were used, the uniforms were different colours and designs and there were different teachers. The school rule was strictly no contact between male and female pupils. Nobody grumbled much about this, having expected it to be the case from the beginning. Instead there was some irresistible attraction to stretching the rule, just bordering on the authority of the masters while not actually going over the line. It was imperative then to have a girlfriend and to walk that walk. Young couples ambling to and from the gates or standing with each other at bus stops cocked a snook at the masters and said, 'I'm on the side of the pupils.'

Solidarity with the boys was demonstrated three times each day by similar strolls at morning, lunch and close of school. That afternoon, leaving his girlfriend at her tram stop, Robert hurried away from boys who wanted to talk about the swimming team and other sports topics with a wave and shouting, 'Got to dash, but tennis on Thursday sounds good. We can confirm tomorrow.'

Speeding home, his haste and a skid brought him close to grief for the second time that day. Arriving safely and his Triumph well stabled in the shed, Robert bounced up the stairs three at a time, pulling his tie loose. School uniform deposited on the bed, he opened the door to his parents' room. In spite of his certainty that he was alone in the house, he always entered this room gingerly, expecting an adult's presence. Perhaps it was how the room smelled of a warm, welcoming aroma distinctive to his parents or the familiar objects on the dresser and by the bedside. It was as if the objects had something of Mother and Father in them or could consume the events in the room only to recount the details to his parents later.

Robert made his selections with care and laid them on the double bed. Pants, chemise, dress and scarf. Almost a full outfit but not complete without stockings and shoes. His feet had outgrown Mother's shoes and denied him a previous pleasure. Stockings he dare not risk in case of ladders or snags in those rare vestments. Father had managed to get a pair and brought them home to Mother as the most special of gifts. They were there now in the drawer, still wrapped in the tissue paper, being kept for Sunday best. Looking at the selection, he returned to the drawer and lifted out a suspender belt.

'Who makes suspenders now?' he wondered. 'After all they are practically redundant. Unless you are going out with an American or a black market dealer, that is. Even then who makes stockings any more? They are bound to run out sometime.' He imagined stocking and suspender factories filled with women in dark boiler suits and scarves round their heads, busy manufacturing parachutes, Army uniforms, kit bags or something and singing along to the Home Station. 'Still, after the war they'll make stockings again, you'll see.' He decided to wear the suspender belt without stockings.

Stripping off his pants and vest, he pulled on the chosen ensemble item by item, all the while watching himself in the three angled mirrors of the dressing table. Once clothed he walked about the room, to and fro in front of the mirrors. He clicked open the wardrobe revealing the long mirror inside the door. Straightening the dress, he moved from room to room. Daring to go downstairs, he walked slowly to the kitchen, ran a cup of water from the cold tap and carried the drink back to his room. Checking the time, he reckoned on having quarter of an hour of freedom left. He knew his anxiety would quicken as the time ticked away and reminded himself of occasions before when people returned home early. Mother would be helping at the National Society for the Prevention of Cruelty to Children (known politely as the NSPCC and less politely as The Cruelty) or attending a Conservative Party do, serving tea and empire biscuits. She would be first back and he could not stand the thought of being confronted by her. Robert trudged back to his parents' room and admired himself in the full-length mirror before turning away to disrobe.

Mother arrived home a little later than he thought. When she bustled in to the living room he was sitting at the table. In front of him lay a closed school book, his collection of Burns' poetry open and he was sketching with a pencil on a piece of paper. Mother asked after his day and whether he had completed his homework. Standing near she could see his sketch was of a woman in a long, flowing dress, low cut at the bodice, and with dark, full, long hair. If Mother had thought to enquire she would have found out that the subject of the sketch was the boy's idea of how Jean Armour looked. As he worked on his drawing he whistled in that mute way, more air than whistle, but the tune was evident and in his head ran the accompanying words:

O my luve is like a red, red rose,
That's newly sprung in June:
O, my luve is like the melodie,
That's sweetly play'd in tune.

As fair art thou, my bonnie lass,
So deep in luve am I,
And I will luve thee still . . .

Robert was dressed as her son, Robert, was expected to dress.

5 The Good Wife and a Witch Hunt Forewarned

The two divinest things a man has got;
A lovely woman in a rural spot.
LEIGH HUNT IN 'THE STORY OF RIMINI'

'The trouble with stereotypes is that they exist,' thought Newman as she unloaded the boot-load of provisions from the car. 'I wish the one about the quality of food in country areas was half accurate.'

For the first few visits to the Cottage she had stuck to her original intention of purchasing everything locally. Living for years on her own, she enjoyed cooking for herself. A pleasure was to spend all afternoon preparing a full menu for dinner that night. A few hours' work followed by a brisk walk would sharpen her appetite for solitary wine, music and food. She had looked forward to local produce in Argyll and realised that a trade-off would have to be made sacrificing peppers, courgettes, chillies and aubergines as exotic, expensive and unavailable. By compensation she expected the indigenous potatoes, kale, carrots and turnip to be delivered daily and so fresh and full of the taste of the earth. The absence of peppers was a small price to pay for venison, Kintyre beef, Islay cheese, salmon, prawns, oysters and scallops. She could survive on that fare quite easily, if the goods had actually been available locally.

The stereotype vouchsafed that the goods would be inexpensive, since country life was meant to be cheap. She understood why there was no low-cost housing. In fact, she took some of the blame on herself as an absentee owner, able to afford premium prices, outstripping rural wages and pricing local people out of the market. In Wales the same phenomenon had brought on arson attacks on empty holiday homes but not here in Argyll. There was talk of some Settler Watch organisation but it seemed to be some half-hearted affair run by one or two social isolates.

The people put up with so little. Few council houses; private property lying empty during winter, collecting high tourist rates for a few months of the summer; a handful of people in every village owning a great deal; young people expected to work for low wages for hard labour on the farms, risking their lives on the fishing boats or displaying efficient servitude in the hotels; large estates where the owners would invite paying guests to shoot the game and howl for maximum penalties if locals dared to poach. A county full of land and a population short of houses. Building on the banks of lochs was forbidden because it would spoil the view and ruin tourism and all the while families lived in damp houses and young people left the area, happier in the bed-sit land of Glasgow or Edinburgh than taking their chances at home where hope for the future was predictable and limited. *Yet* they put up with so little.

Newman had expected wild Highlanders demanding their will and taking no short change from anyone on pain of insurgence, the lighting of beacons, the demonstration of a democracy which bore fools lightly and told them so to their faces. Instead she found a people wild in their cups and mild on their rights. She expected strong silence and found secretive selfishness. The way to success seemed to be: 'tell no one anything and build your nest egg quietly'; in public, to confess a lack of worldliness and be serious and dull at all times; act 'the daft laddie', all the better to outsmart others; be plain and dowdy lest anyone think you successful and try to take it from you by stealth or gossip; be consistent, regular and routine and, above all, keep a low profile.

Before Newman came to this place she had visualised a lean, red-headed race, swathed in tartan plaids, windswept and strong.

Practical: sheltering the stubborn glens by dry-stane dikes; ploughing out the perpetual rye grass and tilling the soil, forcing it against its will to meet their needs; pushing fragile, pug-nosed boats out and into the threatening but fish-full waters, day in and day out, losing their kin and sometimes their lives to bring the catch home; herding their sheep over vast, rock-hewn hills, donating their loneliness and solitude to the cause of survival.

Poetic: damp brows raised from stony furrows to sweep

across sun-touched gorse slopes; turning from dropped nets to follow moon-kissed lochs, yellow and soft, more liquid than mere water; pausing on hill tops, gazing past wandering sheep to witness clouds racing, silver and grey.

Naïve, is how Newman regarded those thoughts. She now understood the significance of the dirk, that short dagger adorning the stocking of every kilt-wearing wedding guest. The dirk was not a noble weapon as suggested by modern ornamentation and the place accorded in formal dress. The dirk was a cheap, sleekit, effective weapon hidden in the sock, waiting for an opportunity for surprise attack. More useful in local, domestic squabbles than in open warfare, this short, stabbing dagger was the modern equivalent of the thug's razor or the football supporter's Stanley knife. Newman thought she understood why the dirk had survived in Highland dress while other accoutrements had been confined to museums.

A vague memory of a history lesson on Scotland years before occurred to Newman. It had been an unusual setting for such a history lesson, being an Army barracks on Bodmin Moor, and the teacher was just as unexpected, being a young Englishman. She could not recall how it had started but placed it in that dimension of National Service involving many hours of boredom, when the soldiers had to make up their own entertainment. Card games, gambling, illicit beer, communal singing all featured but she preferred the story-telling and listened in amazement to the lyrical wealth from otherwise humdrum characters. Newman was a listener but knew how to encourage with a question here, a laugh there, a verbal prod for every occasion.

The young soldier needed little encouragement as he regaled their small group with tales of the North. The English-educated audience knew little about it or had been taught a different variation altogether. The soldier made the history come alive and obviously felt some heroic attachment to the journey of the Scots. So much so, that slices of the telling stayed with Newman long after whole tracts of history, formally taught over years in school and university, had been deleted from her useful memory. There had been no pattern to the stories and they were mixed now in Newman's mind.

Pictish warriors, woad painted, moon worshippers, keeping the Roman legions at bay by sporadic guerrilla tactics – the only country to repel the Romans and not even united at that time.

The tradition of learning and commerce produced the earliest

universities, an influence in the Vatican and a special relationship with many trading countries, especially France. Scots
had languages, in their own right, which remain still – not just
Gaelic but the lowland Scots of Burns and the Doric of the
North-east, derided now as accents and dialects and thrashed
out of children by Scottish teachers in Scottish schools.

English soldiers of an occupying force, raping and murdering
William Wallace's wife, turning him from peaceful country
squire to bitter, angry man intent on freedom; the intelligence of
his victories against much bigger and better equipped armies;
the cruelty and gory public display of his execution.

Scottish mercenaries, merchants, scholars, engineers and
bankers turning up in the history books of nations all over the
planet but the particular association with Russia, Australia,
America and France.

The Highland clearances, when people were run off the land
to make way for the easy, low-maintenance profit of sheep;
men, women and children forced on to beaches by their own
Clan Chiefs (absentee landlords in the main), surviving on
seaweed and starving as they waited for ships which often never
arrived; ships appearing and people being herded like cattle and
treated worse; little more than a white slave trade where many
died en route.

Scottish regiments in the Army of the British Empire and their
reputation as fierce and respected fighters over all the world; the
First World War, when the sight of the infantry marching across
the mud of Normandy, into No Man's Land, kilts swinging as
they advanced, led by a piper whose skirling bagpipes never
ceased, earned the nickname of 'Ladies from Hades' from
enemy troops.

How the Scots were fierce with themselves and had a
treacherous political background; clan would slaughter clan for
reasons going back to some incident centuries before; how the
Clan Chiefs would show allegiance to the side most likely to win
or pay the richest dividends; how Scots so often had power in
their grasp only to let it slip away through greed, internal
dispute or melancholy; the Jacobite rebellion of 1745 fizzling
out at Derby due to an outbreak of discord and homesickness,
only to be routed, slaughtered and enslaved at Culloden and
after; how at Culloden there were as many Scots with the
Butcher of Cumberland as with Bonnie Prince Charlie.

It was about the 1745 uprising that Newman recalled

something which had appalled on the first telling of the story. The clans of Scotland had been divided between Jacobite and Hanoverian alliance. The Jacobite chiefs had pledged support if the Prince would travel from France to lead the forces. In good faith the Prince travelled to Scotland by sea, a hellish, hazardous journey, raised his standard with a small group of French soldiers and waited for the clans to arrive. And waited.

Too many let him down. Before committing themselves, some clans were looking for signals from the most powerful chiefs. A few years earlier a certain chief, a known Jacobite, had been taken to task by the London government. While the official reason was his delay in swearing allegiance to the British Crown, he had faced charges on another matter altogether. The chief stood accused of selling his clan members into slavery, mainly for work in the Americas. Treating free men in this way carried the death penalty. In return for his oath of loyalty to the Crown, King George II let the Clan Chief be. While traditionally a Jacobite, this Chief sat on his hands while others led the charge for freedom. In the meantime, Argyll, Clan Chief of the Campbells and one of the most powerful men in Scotland, waited and watched. Argyll was the first to officially notify London of the Prince's landing in Scotland. Still he waited.

At first, the barbarity of the times had struck Newman, but of stronger impact was the realisation of Argyll profiting from the ensuing chaos in the aftermath of Culloden. While individual clan members had broken ranks to fight the war on the side of the Scots, their Chief sat and waited and, when certain of the victor, rubbed his hands, joined in and received a share of the spoils. Newman thought of this sliver of history each time she drove through Inveraray, passing the splendour of Inveraray Castle, the seat of the Duke of Argyll, Clan Chief of the Campbells.

No wonder these people seemed cautious and suspicious. Newman knew that some lessons take a long time to unlearn. There is a seduction in the mimicking of power, and minor Clan Chiefs abounded. Scotland had not had her revolution, at least not yet. So the people remained cowed and introverted in the matters of change, only expressing themselves and their energy fully in the mists of alcohol or the heat of rumours, gossip and hearsay.

Except in Tarbert, that is. Newman thought the people of that village different somehow. They did not fit in with the rest of

Argyll or with their closest neighbouring communities in particular. Their sense of humour, disregard for office, lust for life, openness and basic humanity marked them as different. It was as if they had been delivered to that cove from elsewhere, bypassing the influence of the greater vastness of the West Highlands. Perhaps by boat across from Ireland or up the Clyde and round the coast, a delivery of Glaswegians bringing the idiosyncratic ways of that city to this corner and no farther. What they thought was funny in Tarbert would be heard as an insult in Lochgilphead. What was a lifestyle in Tarbert would be bohemian degradation in Oban. Newcomers felt welcome in Tarbert but tolerated in Lochgilphead. Newman hoped Tarbert people were different but only time would tell.

Tarbert 'Jakes' were no different when it came to paying high prices for old potatoes, soft carrots and shot onions. Tarbert was a small but busy fishing port, yet the fish available was either priced at extortionate rates or sold in frozen, tasteless lumps you could buy in a poor supermarket anywhere. Hulking lorries with French and Spanish number plates would roll into the village late at night and by early morning, loaded with the crops of the sea, would be on their way again. Buying fruit was a lottery you were most likely to lose when apples turned out to be brown and soft to the core, oranges with a texture of dry rubber and a flavour only slightly reminiscent of citrus. All in all, the diet of poor people.

Newman broke her promise early on and without remorse. She soon realised that Loch Fyne oysters or salmon or whatever, could be purchased more easily away from Argyll. So she filled her car boot with the goods to sweeten her stay in the village and ate out when she could.

She was to dine out that night with a colleague, diverting through the area on her way North. Newman had offered accommodation and dinner at her place. The former was politely refused on the grounds that she 'had a very early start' the next morning. The latter replaced with an offer to treat them both to dinner with 'no washing up'. Newman suspected that the colleague was perplexed by her and wanted to be friendly while keeping a distance. It was what the other did not know that would worry her most. The few associates Newman was required to have regarded her privacy with awe and felt threatened. They knew little of her background and only the basics of her present. While they chatted about wives, husbands, lovers and children she smiled and listened, taking not giving. If they spoke about past projects she asked questions and nodded. On the rare occasions they found themselves socialising alone with Newman, they enjoyed themselves but later realised they had done all the talking and all about themselves. This meeting was a rare event and the woman had time to contemplate the occasion, finding herself wary of being alone with Newman far away from the usual conventions.

They met at the Columba Hotel and ate a meal reeking of the best of Argyll. Newman's enthusiasm for the food was evident and her companion agreed, pleased to see her associate effusive for a change with a 'Highland air must be good for you' comment and a smile. Even as she said this she noted that Newman was talking about the food, something other than herself, and felt as troubled as she had at the start of dinner.

'You are wondering if this is a date,' was the thought which disturbed her most and had done from the time they made the arrangement to meet. 'Just because I'm not married doesn't mean anything, Newman,' was one line she had practised along with, 'I like you Newman, really, but I'm seeing someone else.'

The evening rode on through succulent and filling food and glass after glass of fine wine. They retired to the lounge bar with coffee and brandies to sit by the open fire and look out on the loch. Replete and tired from the food, Newman lit a small, black cigar and seemed to have regained her characteristic reticence. Relieved that the night was coming to an uneventful close and, filled with her natural bonhomie, Newman's companion called for the waitress to thank the chef and passed a separate and generous tip.

The night came to a close when the chef came in to the bar to express gratitude for the gratuity and was held in conversation by Newman's friend and other diners. Talk was about queenies and garlic sauce, Bute versus Islay cheese and the difference between chowder and Cullen skink. Throughout it all Newman sat and smoked silently, watching the conversationalists displaying the epitome of polite behaviour. Unnoticed, she paid close attention to the chef. Her friend kept expressing her amazement on discovering the chef also ran the bed and breakfast establishment where she was to stay, Springside Cottage, a short walk from the hotel. The chef was a handsome woman with a polite east-of-Scotland accent just audible through her educated vowels. She had the controlled beauty of one who might be your favourite teacher, Brown Owl or the owner of the hotel. As the others spoke of food, the climate and the views, Newman looked at the animated face of the chef and thought, not for the first time, 'Bob Pine always lands on his feet. God, he knows how to choose them.'

Jean Pine was busy. She ran Springside Cottage and was cooking at the Columba. She had settled well to life in Tarbert in every sense. Country dancing, bridge, sailing, the Gaelic choir and three fine teenage children. She worked hard, joined in, was sociable and polite. The folk of Tarbert liked and respected Jean and it was easy to see why. Newman recalled Bob Pine and thought of this woman as his wife. In the manner of the art, she intuitively knew how Bob might think of Jean, and words came spilling into her mind:

When first I saw fair Jeanie's face,
I couldna tell what ail'd me:
My heart went fluttering pit-a-pat,
My een they almost fail'd me.
She's aye sae neat, sae trim, sae tight,
All grace does round her hover!
Ae look deprived me o my heart,
And I became her lover.

Watching Jean Pine through a billowing veil of cigar smoke, Newman imagined her and Bob together and her thoughts returned to an earlier subject. 'The people of Tarbert are different, eh? Let us hope so, Jeanie Pine, let us hope so.'

6 Families and Favours

Let us drink to the queer old Dean.
WILLIAM SPOONER ATTRIBUTED

King Edward's School, Birmingham, England. 1945.
It was make your mind up time. Sixth Form would happen in a couple of years and the boys had to make decisions on what subject to major in. The guidance was clear if limited: choose the subject you are best at and intend pursuing at university, college or as a career. The school governors thought it straightforward since each subject was marked to exacting standards so only those capable of study and future success would get through. If a boy wanted desperately to major in English and did not have the grades, that was too bad. If the same boy had his best grades in Classics he would be well advised to pursue Latin and Greek. Whether the emerging adults would be happy in their choice and the direction of their lifetime occupations was of little concern to the governors. In running the school their only endeavour was to produce young adults who passed examinations, who could go on to university or pursue positions in the Civil Service, Armed Forces or other worthy institutions. That is how the school was judged by parents and, of course, future parents willing to pay the fees, buy the uniforms and subscribe to the good reputation of their establishment. Happiness, creativity, satisfaction were mere weak-chinned twaddle.

The school had its rebels – of course it had – and every year, more than ever. Two years before, that boy Kenneth Tynan, though brilliant, was difficult in the worst possible sense of challenging everything except through the proper channels. The masters thought Tynan would do brilliantly or disastrously in life but would never be average. Children were becoming so demanding, expecting so much and lacking the discipline to earn anything by their own endeavour. The masters blamed the American influence: 'Those Yanks coming over here with their money, hair-grease and chewing gum. The Americans show no respect and young men are so easily influenced, more so than ever. The War seems to make things worse rather than better. You expect everyone to show discipline, keep a stiff upper lip and all that, but not the young people today. It is as if they have given up trying and are out for pleasure all the time, enjoying themselves while they can rather than taking things seriously. Really, if the War goes on much longer, goodness knows what will become of this country relying on these young people. They have no form, no backbone.'

But the school would represent standards, tradition and hard work. Life would go on as it had always gone on if the Masters had any influence and, of course, they had some influence. The choice of Sixth Form topic was straightforward really, Robert thought. What he wanted out of life was, simply, as much as possible for the least struggle and he would find the way forward through his Sixth Form choice. He did not care much what the subject was nor did he have any idea or plans on future employment. Mother had made that decision for him already, by all accounts, and he would be a teacher if she had her way. Tina, as Bettina was now calling herself, had already moved on to college and would be teaching soon. He had no difficulty with that career prospect since masters appeared to have a good life, all in all. At least some appeared to have a better life than others and this attracted his concentration. He had not thought of how much teachers earned and assumed that the salary was the same wherever they worked. Still, some masters' black cloaks offered a thin disguise to frayed cuffs and shirt collars which had obviously been turned. Others wore dapper suits, starched collars and gold cufflinks. Some masters walked to school while others sped up in Rovers and Wolseleys. Certain teachers were constantly irritable and angry, picking on the boys for the least misdemeanour (perhaps imagined or anticipated) while others were firm but relaxed, laughing and joking with the boys and sometimes sharing confidences with them. Robert had a sense that these factors were related in a fundamental way, a phenomenon which he did not understand fully but grasped nevertheless.

Aged fifteen going on sixteen, Robert Pine, when asked what he wanted to do when he grew up would, if honest, reply 'be happy'. Like all humans before and after, he had a certain knowledge of what made him happy at that time but was vexed about what would bring happiness to the adult he was to become. Too many others described happiness as responsibility, honour, high office, victory but Robert did not see the world in that way. Too many others identified the examples to be followed in Churchill, Montgomery or maybe Attlee or Stalin. If being serious and forced to choose role models, Robert would select T.S. Eliot or John Betjeman as producing work he could aspire to, if he could be bothered. At fifteen going on sixteen years, Robert Pine could not be bothered that much and chose an example of how to live his life much closer to home.

The mathematics master, Jack Roberts, drove an elegant Rover, owned a sailing boat, wore good suits and liked to tell the boys of his wonderful life. While no pushover, he was an approachable man keen to chat with his pupils and spend time with them away from the formal classroom. Most of the boys enjoyed having Roberts as a teacher simply because he was not an old fuddy-duddy, he had a dry sense of humour, belying his dour demeanour, and treated the older boys with respect, almost as equals. Jack Roberts was a confirmed bachelor but seemed happy, relaxed and comfortable with his life. His combined seriousness and biting wit, if evident in a child, would have been described as cocky or 'too big for his boots'. Roberts was a master and masters could never be 'too big for their boots'. Robert appreciated his teacher's style and thought that would be good enough for him, thank you very much.

In choosing mathematics, Robert Pine gave himself a small problem – it was not his best subject. Fearing he would not achieve high enough examination marks, he approached Jack Roberts for the results of one key test. He had fallen below the grade required to enter Sixth Form. The innocent Robert was puzzled by the master's good humour and never-say-die attitude. The boy also failed to understand the man's suggestion that this question and that had not been scored properly. Surely the master had marked the examination himself? By the time Robert left the classroom his marks had swollen to justify Sixth Form mathematics and he received an invitation to join the master and others for a sail on the Edgbaston reservoir that weekend. Robert was grateful, smiled a great deal but explained he was not free that weekend.

Robert thanked the teacher and left. Hurrying along the corridor he mentally calculated the time. He was running late now but still reckoned he could manage half an hour on his own before Mother returned home. She was doing more work with the Conservative Party and was getting back later and later.

Still, half an hour should be safe and he did not want to take too many risks. Riding his bike on the way home he thought of Jack Roberts and his offer of sailing at the weekend. Normally, he would have jumped at the chance. Sailing was just his cup of tea, swanning about on the water. He remembered a previous holiday when he had gone sailing with Jack Roberts for a week on the Norfolk Broads. He reckoned he had looked the part, decked out in his grey flannels and that baggy white shirt, sketch pad and book of poetry in hand. Rumour had it that Jack let the boys drink beer and would take them to a pub for dinner. There were other rumours too and Robert knew them only too well. Robert knew from experience that sailing was not all the Master got up to on that boat and elsewhere. As he sped homewards, the cycle wheels humming as the air rushed through the spokes, he thought long and hard of those sailing days.

Arriving home in good time, Robert found a note on the kitchen table. It was from Mother, saying she would be home later than usual. Smiling, he set off towards the bedrooms and, keeping time with each step on the stairs, mumbled the words:

Young Peggy blooms our bonniest lass,
Her blush is like the morning,
The rosy dawn, the springing grass,
With early gems adorning.
Her eyes outshine the radiant beams
That gild the passing shower,
And glitter o'er the crystal streams,
And cheer each fresh'ning flower.

Pushing open the door to his parents' room he paused. 'You wouldn't catch me dead on that boat. Not for love nor money.'

~

Oldbury, Midlands, England. 1945.
'The bomb will sort them out,' was Mother's thought on Hiroshima. Those few days between Hiroshima, Nagasaki and the Japanese response took for ever in the minds of some people. The War was not over while it raged in the Far East. Throughout the War the Japanese had been cast in a demonic role with information on the torture of prisoners, kamikaze

pilots, jungle warfare and suicide preferred to surrender, bringing uncertainty and unease now to public consciousness. On 9 August 1945, the Government announced that a second atomic bomb had been dropped on Japan, on the city of Nagasaki. It was the 'ultimate weapon', the people were informed, and the War was bound to come to a close. The propaganda machine had worked too well and amidst the general euphoria, just now and then, a thoughtful, worried face turned to the sky, scanning the horizon for an enemy aeroplane flying from the East with their bomb. Had they not been informed that the Japanese were the most cunning, devious, desperate and determined of Forces, choosing death rather than defeat as a matter of honour? So the people waited on 10 August, 11 August and counting – long days and nights waiting for surrender or retribution. The war years had been full of long periods of sameness and sudden spurts of action, disastrous or victorious. These few days were no different.

During the first few months of the Second World War, people had reassured each other that it would soon be over and the 'boys' would be back home. The weeks after Dunkirk had not gone far in stilling the optimism in some massed, confidence-enhancing exercise. The propaganda spewed out and was consumed willingly and heartily by all, barring the most conscientious objector. Politicians, who had been defaming each other only months earlier, now stood side by side as if their arguments had been healed permanently. The public faced evacuation, rationing, bombing, conscription, cowardice, heroism, bereavement, fire, death and life. The men departed, leaving women and children to wait for letters from anonymous locations and dreaded telegrams from locations known only too well. Life went on not as before but when did it ever?

During the days after Nagasaki, the public face was euphoric but often the private face was reflective. Like a Scottish Hogmanay the revellers looked back to look forward, poised on the cusp of peace and war knowing they had changed, as had life. There were people who could without effort repeat key dates of key events in a cathartic mantra:

3 September 1939   – Declaration of war
29 May 1940   – Dunkirk
2 July 1940   – Germans bomb London in daylight
9 July 1940   – British bomb Germany at night

10 May 1941	– Luftwaffe destroys House of Commons
10 May 1941	– Rudolph Hess lands in Scotland
7 December 1941	– Pearl Harbour
8 December 1941	– USA declares war on Japan
11 December 1941	– USA declares war on Germany and Italy

and so on, through every month of every year, event after event. The lists marked the calendar of their lives suspended in some ways, accelerated in others, never to be the same again. The lists welded a thin, protective veneer over the pain of change and loss. For many there was a realisation that they had lived through a time of secrets disguised as an age of openness. Secrets are necessary in war, 'loose talk cost lives' so 'beware the enemy within'. They were about to learn secrets of war that would blunt their innocence forever.

Public secrets: concentration camps killing millions of Jews, trade unionists, gypsies, homosexuals, disabled and mentally ill people ignored by the Allies as lacking strategic importance; propaganda, cleared by Churchill, showing fair-skinned, naked women being mounted by dark-skinned men, a message to the German troops about their wives and the enforced immigrant workers back home; massacres too many; madness in the Government; frozen bodies on the doorstep of Leningrad; Swiss bankers and the gold of the dispossessed; the Bomb, of course, the Bomb which would end the war and threaten the world for ever and a day.

Private secrets: lovers taken; murders committed; cowardice and fear; pleasure at killing; money stolen; relief at being apart; hearts broken; laughs laughed while others were being killed; pleading with God to kill Germans, Italians, Japanese, Russians, Poles, French, Indians, Americans, Australians, Canadians, other British soldiers, just anyone else to let your loved ones come home safe; sexual encounters of the briefest kind; and so on. Just another ordinary time, in other words.

Robert Pine did not keep lists of dates in his head, not about the War at any rate. He had been too busy growing up from an awkward, enthusiastic child to a smooth and mannered young man. All around him there had been change and stability in that curious mixture, possible in some families. The whole family had moved on while remaining the same in fundamental character.

Tina had gone to college to train as a teacher, thereby

meeting Mother's will. An intelligent, energetic young woman, she did well in everything. During a period when women were engineers, doctors, tram drivers, pilots, soldiers and more, Tina pursued a traditionally respectable profession. Family debates and discussions were not necessary as Tina pursued what Mother wanted and a career where women were welcome, had been welcome for years. Tina teaching would not challenge the family's standing or aspirations. Nor would teaching pull the young woman down a route shaping or limiting her life in any way her parents might fear. Tina could meet a young man, a student or teacher, marry and settle down to a life of suburban regularity. Tina could stay single, continue teaching, be well off in her own right and become a solid and dignified figure in the community she served. If the young woman's life was to evolve in the latter direction, it would be unlikely that she would move schools, ever. It was expected that she would serve the public from the same classroom in the same school, generation after generation. Mothers would bring their young offspring to enrol in her class and tell their little Betty or Jimmy that they had sat in this very room and been taught by Miss Pine.

The War had done little to shake the fortitude of Miss Bettina Pine. She was intelligent, strong and sure and made her parents feel proud and safe. The future was in good hands with Tina Pine. She was an example to them all.

At home in 11 Edward Road, Oldbury, Mrs Pine was Mother but in the intimacy of her relationship with Father and a few select others, Mother was Eva Pine. Eva was a dynamo, full of energy, orders, certainty and direction. Emerging from a family of engineers, male of course, but she being one of the few women, Eva knew what was right and made sure others followed suit. The children were never in doubt that Mother was to be obeyed, double quick style. Eva had continued through the War years to keep the home spick and span and in tip-top shape. That was her role, after all, and she did it well. Eva Pine had too much energy for looking after the house. While others had, for generations, struggled with the daily, weekly, grinding routine when carpets had to be beaten by hand, floors washed on knees, brasses polished, beeswax rubbed and rubbed into wood, and windows washed with vinegar, Eva had energy and time to spare.

When Eva Pine was first married, she had been expected to

keep home and there was an end to it. Those women suggesting that they could or should do something else were either driven by poverty or somehow morally suspect and Eva was neither. Certain activities were acceptable in the most polite circles – charity and helping out at organised activities. For the charity, Mother chose the NSPCC and supported them in their work caring for orphans, battered children, poverty-stricken families and so on. The War had brought with it a heightening of such social problems and help was provided by the charities, their workload soaring over those years. For 'helping out at organised activities', read making the tea, serving at fund raisers, sitting quietly on committees, typing the minutes. Eva Pine chose the Conservative Party. For the past five years she had indeed made the tea, just increasingly so. When there was any event or any task, Eva would be there organising and helping. The local Conservative Association had come to rely on her, particularly with so many of their members in the Armed Forces. The Conservative Party did not know how they could manage without their Eva Pines.

The world knew Father as William Pine, a good sort from an extended family dominated by sisters and aunts, strong women all. He had continued to work as the Personal Assistant to the Director of Birmingham and Midlands Omnibus Co. a private bus service provider and one of the largest in England. The position paid well, carried status and benefited from William's neat organisational style, easy-going manner and gentle creativity. William Pine was not a Personal Assistant, that was just what he did for a living. William Pine was an artist. Father drew, read and wrote. A gentle, poetic man he was trapped into a way of life demanding that he earn a wage, hold a position and face the world in a particular way. He faced the world and his family with acumen and style.

In a protected post and too old for active service, the main personal impact of the War on William Pine was his service as an Air Warden. Equipped with a metal hat, arm band, kit bag, whistle and torch, he patrolled the night-time streets checking that blackout blinds were down, car lights were off and no fire was showing. During air raid alerts he would rush around and make sure that families were taking shelter, hiding from the danger. On sighting enemy aircraft, he and his peers would telephone ahead or to Command, warning of an attack. There was an irony in William Pine's role during those war years that a man so entranced with beauty and light should spend so much energy on danger and darkness.

William was devoted to Eva in an open way, uncommon in those hard-edged times. He did not or, perhaps, could not hide his feelings for his wife from the gaze and knowledge of others. The War had nothing to do with the depth of William's feelings. His was not a fly-by-night flash of emotion fuelled by fear and circumstances. He loved her before the War and loved her still. In his love, as in many other aspects of his life, the War was irrelevant to the father of the family.

Father and son had a great deal in common through their artistic temperaments, creative aptitudes, easy-going natures and a tendency to idealise and admire women. In Father's case the admiration for the female form was specific and targeted at Mother, his own Eva. In Robert's case, he simply admired girls and now young women. The years of war had heralded changes in Robert in that he had grown up as his view of the world expanded. Robert had become confirmed in his love of art, his fascination with the poetic phrase and his enjoyment of drama as participant more than observer. He had become himself, just more so.

At the start of the Second World War, Robert Pine was a child who played with children. By the end of the Second World War, Robert Pine was a young man who associated with young women. In his sense of self, the War was irrelevant to Robert Pine. Like father like son.

Poised now between the atomic bomb and what was to come next, Robert Pine reviewed what was important to him. He did not look to the sky for signs of hostile aircraft but would look upwards to admire the colour of the clouds. He did not count the days since Nagasaki nor did he rush home to listen to Churchillian announcements on the wireless. He was moved and troubled by the horrors of Belsen, Treblinka and Auschwitz but was not obsessed by the 'Final Solution'. Robert Pine had a personal worry or two which he returned to during those private moments which describe the introspection of most teenagers. Robert Pine was beginning to realise that he was not good at mathematics, that maybe he had made a mistake.

On 14 July 1945, the Japanese surrendered and the Second World War was all but over. Teenagers throughout the western world celebrated along with everyone else and then returned to their concerns about their looks, their haircuts, their exams, their spots, their futures and all the rest of that endless list of questions marking the movement through the final stages of childhood and the new beginning of adulthood. The Second World War was not that important for Robert Pine. He had a great deal in common with young people all over the world.

7 A Warning

When shall we three meet again
In thunder, lightning, or in rain?
SHAKESPEARE IN 'MACBETH'

The pub reminded Newman of a drinking den in some inner-urban scheme of slums. It had the same sort of feel to it – sleazy and dangerous.

The Victoria Hotel was the place in Tarbert where you could get anything you wanted and, sometimes, things you had not requested. Built on two levels, with a dance floor next to the main area, the place was often crowded with people intent on having what they wanted. On the nights the fishermen got paid there would be bloody fights, with knives common in the affrays. On weekend dance nights, drunken underage girls would be escorted out into the dark by older men who would return later, alone and boastful. Every day and night, certain characters were always there, propping up the same, precise location. It was as if they lived there, having no need to leave.

Loud country and western music was the theme tune and the customers seemed to take the lyrics to heart, using them as a plan by which to model their lives. If you were a stranger to Tarbert, this was not the place to enter for a quiet drink and a snack.

At a small table, in a smattering of space between the inglenook and glass side-door sat Newman and a man. They sat slightly apart, leaning back into their chairs but, nevertheless, sustained conversation while looking as if they were neither acquainted with or interested in each other. The man, with his wife and family, had moved to the area three years before so that the children could grow up in a safe and fertile environment and he, their father, could expand his work as an artist with no distractions save the beauty of the land.

The two had met on a walk up by the castle, high above Tarbert. The hill there was flattened at the top and made for an easy, circuitous route through the ferns and around the battlements. There, far above, the day-to-day life of the village was unseen and unheard. The occasional shrill cry of a bird warned passers-by to stay away from her nest. Newman's knowledge was weak on birds and plants and, in the unavoidable confrontation of hearing that pained cry, she regretted never having the patience or the inclination to learn more of this, decidedly inhuman, aspect of nature. For the umpteenth time in her life she was acknowledging to herself that she would never learn more about birds, when she was startled by the tread of boots close by.

The fellow stroller appeared to know that she was listening to the bird and rather than a greeting, started a conversation with, 'Makes you think, what is she saying . . . the bird?'

'How do you know it's a she and not a show-off he?' was Newman's reply.

Two consecutive questions make it hard to avoid a fight or a dialogue. So the two ramblers, choosing conversation, followed the path round the hill top debating the differences, if any, in characteristic traits between male and female. It was apparent to both that they favoured the perceived nurturing traits of the female, till Newman had to own up that she, for one, was not nurturing nor into nature and she resented such classification. Her companion retorted with the revelation that all his adult life he had resented being told that he had a strong feminine side to his character just because he was supportive, a listener, gentle and creative. He was who and how he was, and there was an end to it.

Confessions and debate can solder people together and by the time they returned to the castle, each thought they understood a great deal about the other. Pausing to catch their breath and to ingest the views over Cowal and west to the hills of Arran, Newman's friend nodded at the crumbling rocks of the fortress and gave a gift of a story about the days of Cromwell when Roundheads occupied the one-time home of Bruce, the fugitive. In spite of the military precision and order dictated by Parliament, Tarbert men raided the citadel. Apart from barrels of gunpowder, the Tarbert tykes stole a substantial quantity of cheese and twenty-six bags of biscuits. As the two new friends descended the path, they joked about how popular history could have been so different if only there had been a heavy tax on the food.

'Boston had its Tea Party but Tarbert brought the cheese and biscuits.'

'The Tarbert Savoury Snack.'

And so the friendship was formed and cheese or biscuits lasted as a recurring theme joke over many meetings and several years.

The two friends met for the occasional drink. Newman resisted all invitations for dinner and met the man's wife and children only by accident, in the street or in front of the shops. On such occasions she was polite but circumspect. Eventually she thought that further rejection of offers would be downright rude and she found herself in the family's company at a performance of the local Gaelic choir. Attending such occasions had been on her list of intentions when she bought the Cottage in Argyll but she found herself, four or five years on, having failed to achieve most of her aspirations. The night out killed at least two birds with the one stone and Newman took consolation in feeling that, even if the singing was poor or the language inaccessible, she could, at least, feel good about herself.

The performance was invigorating and moving. There was a strange sense of *déjà vu* as the choir sang in harmony, the voice music filling the air with dreams of lonely islands, seal people, happy celebrations or love, while the individual members were recognisable from the street, the doctor's surgery, the newsagent shop. Newman's reveries had been diverted by a compulsion to watch the performers closely and she worked her way down the rows making mental notes of those she knew and what she knew about them, before moving on to the next singer. This was partly a personal test of how well she had taken the villagers in and partly an old habit of watching people when they cannot watch back. Robert and Jean Pine were on the stage, for all the world singing like native-born speakers of God's own language. Newman, the cynic, questioned whether they were miming or just humming along. She thought of Robert's sometimes plummy public school accent, the educated Edinburgh tones of Jean and how they contrasted with the lilt of the Scots, especially those from the islands.

After the concert, the audience joined with the performers for tea and to offer congratulations. Hedged in by people on all sides, Newman stood and balanced her cup and saucer while chatting with her friend and his wife. Newman deployed an old trick and tuned in and out of the conversations around and behind her while showing no visible signs of distraction. To her side she overheard the breathy, congested tones of an old woman's voice congratulate Bob Pine, not on his singing but for wearing the kilt every day and, 'Not just for special. Braw.'

Weeks later, sitting in the spit-and-sawdust atmosphere of the Victoria Hotel, Newman thanked her friend for arranging tickets to the concert and raised the subject of Bob and Jean Pine. Her friend was conversant with all things local and in this matched the villagers. Newman was informed that the Pines had learned their Gaelic phonetically. Her friend described the process in detail and revealed, without any surprise for Newman, that he had dabbled in the process, picking up a few phrases. The Pines had learned Gaelic specifically for the choir which placed some doubt on their ability to converse in the language. However, the speed and fluency required by the songs was substantial and the couple's dedication and application had won them many friends.

Newman's friend seemed anxious, not his customary state, and soon revealed the cause of his edginess by blurting out that he and his wife had decided to leave Tarbert. Typical of how their relationship had developed, Newman's face winced into a disapproving frown which, in others, would usually preface a comment. Newman sat, frowned, listened and said nothing. She was accustomed to the path her friend's reasoning pursued and it was a winding, tortuous route at times. For as yet unfathomable reasons, he jumped straight from his announcement to observations on Tarbert life. He spoke of the business families who ran the fishing boats, the hotels and the shops; how they bobbed and weaved along with the best entrepreneurs and were extending to fish farms, haulage and tourism; the village's unique set of unwritten inheritance rules, incomprehensible to the outsider, ensuring wealth and property stayed in the families who would stay in Tarbert; the contrast between the mansions along the shore and the council houses at the back of the village. While even moderate economists would predict that such juxtaposition of have and have-nots would bring on resentment, the village was a classless place.

Tarbert had its other side, her friend vouchsafed. When he had first moved to Argyll he had worried over and then dismissed the comments, by those from surrounding towns, about the dark side to the village. On learning he was moving to Tarbert, strangers volunteered that the Jakes were all on social security, the place had a high number of single parents, the children were wild and untamed and alcohol played a prominent role in many villagers' lives. Worse was said such as references to the extent of in-breeding, the level of crime and the sporadic violence on the streets.

'Bitter, superstitious comments from people with nothing better to think about,' was how Newman's friend dismissed these comments. Then someone had told him stories of a car-key club where partners were swapped, the middle-class version of what happened in some council houses minus the gamesmanship. Allegations about a local minister seducing young men of the area and everyone knowing but choosing to leave well alone. Insinuations about medical disorders, rare throughout the country but common in Tarbert, proving that there was some genetic fault caused by incest or, more esoterically, that the badness was emerging – witchcraft being practised over the generations and practised still.

The slander went on and on and still Newman's friend decided on the only sensible course – to make up his own mind. He had never been invited to wife swapping or a witches' coven. He paused to add 'worse luck', with a smile. Tarbert had its problems but it had its good points too. He reminded Newman of her interest in Bob and Jean Pine and opted to use them as one convenient example.

The Pines had moved to the village five years before. They had worked hard at their shop and bed and breakfast business but their major contribution to Tarbert had been to the social and cultural side. The Pines were prominent and consistent players in the choir, poetry club, Scottish country dancing nights, bridge schools, sailing and every dance, public event or fund raiser. He was now known affectionately as Kiltie and at worst locals thought him a little eccentric for his constant wearing of the kilt – a readily accepted peculiarity.

The Pines were givers and contributed to that part of Tarbert life difficult to emulate elsewhere even in much larger towns. Yet only a few years ago they were newcomers with different accents and ways. Jean's three children had to adjust, and quickly. Children could be cruel and never more so when confronted by someone with a distinct accent who had no friends, big brother or hulking cousin to protect them. He had learned from a teacher friend that one of the lassies, Jackie, he thought, had scored two per cent in her first history exam. Why? Because she had been taught in a Yorkshire school to a different curriculum and could not know the answers to any of the questions. There she was, a bright fourteen-year-old, moving from a class of twenty-six pupils in Harrogate to Tarbert where there were fewer than twenty-six in her year. Fourteen is a sensitive age. The boy, Campbell, had been at primary school and the younger the children the more vicious they can be, Tarbert youngsters being no exception. In spite of all of these hurdles, the Pines had not only settled and been given a place in Tarbert, they had also given back.

But Newman's friend was concerned with how he saw aspects of Tarbert developing. He had come here from another place, where growing up was full of too many dangers for his children, and he had moved to give them a better life. Now he felt that the decay of the cities was moving out and threatening to engulf the country and spoil his idyll. He had an image, comical in its origin but real and threatening to his mind, of a cartoon map of the country and across it sweeping a growing bleak grey mass, marked with skull and crossbones.

'*Dad's Army*. The opening of the television programme with the theme tune and the titles? Remember?' asked Newman's friend. 'When the swastika had overwhelmed Europe the cheeky chappie of the Union Jack would stick its tongue out across the Channel – free, impertinent, but not very strong. That's the countryside in Scotland. Soon the drugs scene here will be as bad, worse probably, than in Glasgow a hundred miles down the road.'

The man was frightened of the inevitable, in Newman's view. She also thought his analysis was wrong and it was not so much a case of being invaded as of importation. When she drove up to Argyll late on a Friday or Saturday evening, she was puzzled by the extent of the traffic going in the opposite direction. Then she found out, through osmosis rather than by a telling, that many of these cars were filled with young adults heading towards Glasgow or Edinburgh to go clubbing, drinking and partying. Conversely, as she drove out of the county late on a Sunday, the same hedonists would be driving home, now weary and already looking forward to the following weekend. Then there were those young people who left the area never to return but who kept in touch with their friends back home. In tenement flats all over the Scottish urban scene, temporary

Argyll communities would spring up for parties and concerts with the guests driving down to stay. Christmas, New Year, weddings, funerals, music festivals and other occasions would witness an influx back of the ex-pats all geared up for days and nights of good fun and happy to share their new-found pleasures and tastes with their old friends. Newman understood that the young would ensure that the world was a shrinking place and Scotland a mere microcosm, for good or for ill.

Newman's friend had determined to leave Tarbert and Argyll. While others taking this journey tended to return to their place of origin, this good family was heading to the perceived shelter of the Western Isles. Stretching out like a sea break, protecting the mainland from the ravages of the Atlantic, these islands looked to be as remote from the centre as could be found. Newman decided not to forewarn her friend of the high alcohol dependence among the population and the scenes of stupefied teenagers wandering the streets of Stornoway most nights. She decided that it was the quest that was important to this man, the knowledge that he had tried to find the best place for his family.

Saying goodnight outside the hotel, Newman decided to take in the night air before returning to her car and the drive home. Walking up Barmore Road, heading out of the village and leaving the milk-top rustle of the yachts behind, she turned left and started the gentle climb up Lady Ileene Road. The narrow street was bordered on either side by houses of a magnitude and spread to indicate wealth and well-being. From one house the rhythmic lowing of fiddles and soft drums drifted across the night, touching a sense of sad purpose and drawing a peaceful tone to Newman's mood. Pausing by the war memorial at the top of the street, she walked forward to the edge of the grass overlooking the village and the bay. Newman watched the wind draw ripples and foam in the waves like lumps of meerschaum floating on the loch. A mist veiled Cowal and a low breeze was pushing clouds across the water in patches of grey air. Newman thought of Robert and Jean. She could still make out their cottage, Springside, down the Harbour Road and she wondered what was happening in there now. Were they sitting on battered easy chairs by the fireside, listening to classical music on the radio and reading of their respective fascinations? Did Jean share Robert's love of poetry and of Burns in particular? Would they be sitting now reciting a favourite poem? Newman thought and spoke the words out loud:

O Thou, that in the Heavens does dwell,
Wha, as it pleases best Thysel',
Sends ane to Heaven an' ten to Hell,
A' for Thy glory,
And no for onie guid or ill
They've done afore Thee!

She sniggered and apologised to Robert and Jean for the inappropriateness of the poem chosen, but excused herself as having a limited range when it came to the other Bard.

Or were they even in Springside at all? From the description of their involvement in the cultural life of the village they were more than likely to be out at a ceilidh, teaching reels to a class of women partnering each other for lack of men; at someone's home discussing poetry and reading their own compositions; at choir practice; playing bridge; in Glasgow at a performance of Scottish Opera; or joining in on one of the hundred social occasions which must arise from such an active role in the community.

Robert and Jean had managed to do more than settle. They were players in Tarbert life. That side of life in Tarbert which Newman's friend admired and would miss. That aspect of life in Argyll which made the county rich and produced people of education and class. They had achieved this involvement in the first few years, the very period when those new to the area suffered most and often left. Newman's friend had been envious of Robert and Jean in the best possible sense of wishing the same feeling of belonging for himself and his own family. Newman was not so sure. Standing on the lip of the village watching the smoke lick the roofs and tasting the smell of burning wood, she worried for the husband and wife, Robert and Jean. There would be no hiding place for them here at any time. The viciousness of people was universal, in Newman's opinion, and those who did not belong were always an easy target. She stood and looked across at the lights of Springside and sent a wordless warning to Robert and Jean: 'The first time you step out of line . . . the first time they believe you to be odd . . . the first time you choose to be too different . . . they will simply crucify you.'

8 Young and Wild at Heart

Youth is a blunder;
Manhood a struggle;
Old Age a regret.
BENJAMIN DISRAELI IN 'CONINGSBY'

Bodmin Moor, Cornwall, England. 1950.
Robert hated being a soldier more than he had imagined. As he tackled his basic training with the feigned enthusiasm of the recruit, he knew he would make a poor soldier. He had not questioned serving in the Armed Forces, since his generation had grown up with the prospect and why should he waste time worrying about the inevitable. National Service was child's play compared to what had been required of people only four or five years earlier. Any teenager careless enough to express displeasure, or even an alternative proposal for national security, was soon put down by morbid reminders of an all too recent time.

During the new era, the fresh start of creating a country 'fit for heroes', those young adults were bound to meet someone whose relatives had died, been blown apart, made homeless, orphaned, left disabled or worse and made to feel weak and disloyal by their protest. When complaint was considered to be useless, the logical response was to accept your lot. Robert wasted no time on such grumps but did not like the thought of 'biting the bullet' or 'buckling down'. He was doing what he always did – what was expected of him, but in the easiest possible way.

The good news was that the 'readiness for war' state of affairs had been eased slightly and the time he was required to serve had been reduced to eighteen months. As with many happy chances in his life, Robert accepted his good fortune as one with the grace to believe that luck would always follow him. He had few views on the threat of war with the USSR and, like most of his contemporaries, was a little confused, though not greatly concerned, by the dynamics of an enemy becoming an ally becoming an enemy. He had grown up from a nine-year-old to a fourteen-year-old during a world war and become accustomed to war. Now there was a Labour Government, a National Health Service, a Welfare State and promises of a new future, free of hunger, disease and poverty. Winnie was speaking of an Iron Curtain and nobody was promising peace in our time – no one would, ever again.

If Robert had been asked for the major events of the last few years he would have mentioned Laurence Olivier's film of *Hamlet*, Tennessee Williams' play *A Streetcar Named Desire* or Eugene O'Neill's *The Iceman Cometh*. He may have mentioned T.S. Eliot's *Four Quartets*, and Benjamin Britten's *Violin Concerto* was growing on him. Others might have listed the events in Palestine, the creation of the United Nations Organisation or the nationalisation of the Bank of England.

Robert had difficulty in remembering the date he started his National Service but he could recite great screeds of Burns, learn the lines of a play or discuss at length the emotions stirred in him by a particular piece of music. Four or five years earlier the Army would not have cared much for Robert Pine's approach. They would simply have bashed him into shape and used him as a foot soldier in the infantry. The Army was still stuck with him and those like him but now had more of a need for his skills and aptitudes.

Robert had volunteered for the Army Educational Corps. In spite of his lack of interest in mathematics he had managed to demonstrate possession of a good brain and obtain a place at university, delayed while he did his bit for King and Country. The Army accepted him on these terms and would use him to train those war-hardened Non Commissioned Officers queuing up to be demobbed. These NCOs had to be retrained to fulfil useful roles in a country at peace. Their knowledge of armaments, endurance under fire, capacity to follow orders, ability to watch their comrades die and still go on – all of this was more or less redundant. Now they had to have a basic education, sit and pass exams, emerging into this new society as contributing, certificated adults. The veterans were rushed through crash courses and the Army needed people to teach them. Training teachers had not been a priority over the previous few years, thus Robert and other fresh-faced school leavers found themselves on their own personal crash courses on basic infantry training and prompt promotion to Sergeant, the grade required to be teachers in the Army.

The Green Jackets Rifle Brigade had a heroic ring to its name, history and place in the mythology of combat. Robert understood all that but the significance of this regiment for him was that, in the sleepy town of Winchester, they tried to teach him and others how to walk, shoot, speak and follow orders. He hated the square-bashing and repetitive routine of those months but worse was to come. Or so he thought when he was told he was to finish his training on Bodmin Moor, Cornwall. Robert's head filled with expectations of running across the moor, heavy pack strapped to his back, while the whoosh and bang of big guns rattled his inner ear, driving away the capacity for quiet contemplation. He anticipated drab scenery with days of rain and drizzle pushed by the steady wind in horizontal drafts. The barracks would be miles from the nearest town which he expected to be small with few facilities beyond a pub, post office and tea room for passing tourists or ramblers. Instead, he found himself by the coast, during the most glorious of summers, in the company of troops keen to create their own entertainment.

Robert and colleagues set up a production of Terence Rattigan's *French Without Tears*. Most of the players were conscripts, biding their time till adult life and ambitions commenced for real, while a minority were regulars including one female officer. Throughout his life, Robert had become accustomed to all parts being played by boys, particularly at public school. He loved acting and would fill any role. Previously he had found himself envious of other boys chosen to play the prominent female characters, officially believing such to allow greater scope for expressive acting skills. Preparing for this play, he recalled being a twelve-year-old schoolboy, annoyed that another boy had been called on to play a minor female part even though Robert's character was more significant and with lines, which the other lacked. No cause for aggravation on this occasion, as the female actors took the female roles.

The play was a success and, in the fashion of amateur players as well as the relationship between the Armed Forces and the public at that time, they toured with the production to surrounding venues, utilising the proliferation of village and church halls. Such activities were a diversification from the role of teaching classes of men usually reluctant, older and more worldly-wise than any of the teachers.

The play was put on in Newquay, at that time a picturesque and tranquil little town. Many towns, particularly by the coast, were temperance-led, having no truck at all with alcohol, but not so Newquay. After a well-received performance, the cast retired to a local hostelry to toast the success and soothe tonsils with warm ale. Many of the young conscripts were novices in the art of consuming alcohol while remaining sober. Some understood this and limited their intake to a couple of beers. Robert was in an expansive and celebratory mood not conducive to abstinence or self-discipline. Later that night, as the troupe made their way back to camp, travelling in the back of large, juddering khaki-coloured lorries, Robert sat next to a lady officer and held forth on Rattigan's work and how they could improve it. The motion of the truck was irregular and occasionally violent as it lurched into potholes and swung round bends. The soldiers sat on hard benches facing each other and there was a great deal of animated banter, shouted at full volume to overcome the roar and crunch of the engine and gears. Some of the passengers sat quietly, fatigued by the long day and the substantial libation. One soldier, a young regular, sat silently and looked straight ahead at Robert and the lady officer. It appeared as if he was trying to divine the essence of the conversation since he was unlikely to hear it over the commotion of the vehicle and the more boisterous travellers. The young regular's head nodded with the bumping of the truck, causing some comrades to pause and ask him if he was feeling well. He reassured them with a nod and an enthusiastic thumbs up, returning his posture and gaze to the original position.

All at once the soldier was on his feet, causing his colleagues to start. At first they thought their earlier concerns had been accurate and a combination of poor suspension, travel sickness and large quantities of beer were taking their toll. They quickly realised that though they were correct, they had guessed the wrong victim.

Without warning, Robert Pine had turned and spewed heftily over the lady officer. As the soldiers supported the slumping Robert, he vomited again with copious liquid bile finding its target. Robert Pine was a gentleman with manners and managed to apologise even as he was sick again, this time out of the back of the truck. The accident was of some personal embarrassment to Robert and his comrades would tease him about it repeatedly. Most of them assumed that Bob Pine, in his cups, had gained sufficient Dutch courage to chat up the lady officer. Whether or not she was young, attractive, approachable or otherwise was irrelevant since she was a woman among a multitude of men, thereby deserving special attention. From that night, some of the young conscripts thought highly of Bob Pine for his combined gall in making overtures to an officer and the embarrassment of his unplanned bull's-eye of an evacuation. Bob Pine, on the other hand, recalled being happy and drunk.

~

Bodmin Moor, Cornwall, England. 1950.
The summer was over and Robert Pine and colleagues were to move on. They had made many friends, becoming closer to each other as strangers tend to when forced into an alien situation. National Service had interfered with all of their lives and while few openly complained, privately most wished for the time past. At summer's end, the imminence of their group disbanding brought a sadness mixed with pleasure at the marking of the passing of time towards their personal plans, and the future.

The members of the Education Corps were to be posted wherever the Army had uncertificated NCOs. Most would be sent to garrison towns like Aldershot, York or back to Winchester. Some would be sent abroad and, while excited by the prospect, the realistic among them were also a little fearful since their destinations were likely to be places where disputes continued. The world was no longer at war but there were still wars in the world. Sergeant Robert Pine was told to expect a posting to West Africa. He did not expend much energy on what awaited him there. The posting would be an order but would result in a visit to a part of the world he considered to be exotic. In truth, he would be journeying into a place of bloody turmoil and interracial warfare.

Sergeant Pine was ordered to Plymouth, his eventual port of departure. On this occasion he would be given the full range of chemical and medical protection against diseases, poisonous bites and nipping insects rife in Africa. Robert was excited by the journey since it marked the certainty of his departure abroad, the Army not being known to waste good medical attention on conscripts. Following the Plymouth trip he would be allowed home immediately on embarkation leave, Army jargon for a rest before the storm.

The Education Corps were all allowed a period of home leave. As with people everywhere, they had all set down roots in their temporary billets in Bodmin. Some had photographs of sweethearts prominently displayed on the lockers by their bedsides. Others, not so advanced, had black-and-white portraits of parents, brothers and sisters. One had the picture of his dog, the being he missed most during his sojourn away from home. In the lockers, hidden from easy public view, was a mixture of the day-to-day necessities such as shaving brush and razor to the front and, to the rear, little slices of private life, too intimate to share with comrades or too personal to display to the inspecting officers. Now and then, a soldier would hide contraband goods in his locker such as a quarter bottle of whisky or a girlie magazine. Whisky has not changed much but the girlie magazines were almost innocent with nipples obscured by black bands or airbrushed out as if the models were missing this part of their anatomy. Getting closer to the sacrosanct were scented missives from lovers or carefully hidden condoms. Erotic stories were occasionally in evidence. These were often hand written, being a transcript from a book or having been made up by a person unknown, then copied and circulated. Possession of these goods carried a range of punishments from a bawling out to a long day peeling spuds in the cookhouse. Regular inspections by the Sergeant Major, announced and expected as well as unannounced and sudden, were designed to find these goods – or so the new recruits believed. For the brass to find these items was one thing but they always knew that they were there in those metal lockers. Soldiers have been soldiers and men have behaved as men for ever. If they wanted to find something in your locker, your knapsack or pocket, they would find it and never be surprised, let alone shocked.

Robert was packing in preparation for his furlough and he was worried. After an initial period of adjustment, he had with difficulty and not inconsiderable inventiveness, stored one or two precious articles among his Army possessions. Months into the regime he had worked up to some confidence that these items were safe from the inspectorial eyes. He had never quite managed to relax the stealth he had been obliged to deploy and suffered an anxious moment every now and then. He could manage though, as long as the regime did not change. Things were certainly about to change and he feared spot checks ensuring that none of the conscripts had collected mementoes of their stay on Bodmin – the Army were always suspicious of the trivial. He had decided to take pre-emptive action. Rolling the sensitive items into a ball and shoving them deep into his pocket he walked briskly through the camp to the refuse dump. Checking no one was watching he bent as if to tie his boot lace and standing up stuffed the deposits deep into the rubbish.

On his way home from Plymouth days later, he felt some relief at being free of any incriminating goods. He managed a wry smile as he imagined the bully-voiced Sergeant Major lecturing the next delivery of recruits on the discipline required and strictures imposed. Going on to remind the awkward squad that they were no longer in their mothers' care and, unlike those saintly madonnas, he knew what young men were really like and would be wise to all their tricks. He had been in the Army twenty years man and boy and had seen it all more than once. So, they had better wise up quick because he was on to them.

Robert smirked at the thought of nervous youngsters, standing to attention, stiff and tense, but giving the game away by the gulping of their Adam's apple. He regretted the waste of disposing of his intimate goods. They had not been easy to obtain in the first place and he had felt like a sneak thief buying them in the shop. He simply applied his acting repertoire, taking on the cloak of someone purchasing a gift for a girlfriend. The older shop assistant had looked at him as if she knew the real purpose of the clothes and once or twice he had felt his face redden. He repeated a mantra in his head, convincing himself that she was a sad old snob who looked down her nose at everyone. The three garments had cost him twenty minutes of sweat and nervousness, all ending in their disposal buried deep in those bins of rotting rubbish. He knew he would be compelled to go through it all again and hoped this time he would have more opportunity to wear the clothes.

Perhaps in West Africa, now he was a sergeant, he would be allocated his own room and some blessed privacy. He had heard that you were treated well out there with servants, room service and gin on the verandah before dinner. He half suspected that the old soldier who told him these tales was lying but he preferred to hold on to the image. Then it occurred to him that out there in the tropical heat of the jungle and coffee plantations, there would be very few English women and, therefore, few shops for English women. He would need to plan ahead if he could. 'Strategy, tactics and planning,' they had barked at him during his Army training. Well, he would deploy such devices now. He thought about the task ahead off and on, all the way home to Oldbury.

When Sergeant Robert Pine arrived home, a letter awaited him. His posting to West Africa had been cancelled. He was posted to Bicester, Oxfordshire.

~

Birmingham, England. 1951.

All over the world there were hot spots likely to flare up to full-scale war at any time. The unification of nations into two major sides during the Second World War had been diluted and in the wheeling and dealing that followed it, old scores and disharmony, stretching back centuries, emerged with a vengeance. Communism had always been feared but now it was a major force, battle fit and racing for its own atomic bomb. Korea bubbled and China postured. African countries demanded their independence from the British Empire. In the Middle East, ancient demarcations drew out war from a scuttling guerrilla affair, escalating week after week. Peace had a narrow, tenuous foothold.

Along with every other ex-National Service soldier, sailor or airman, Robert Pine was obliged to serve in the Reserves. With an affair like the Territorial Army, they maintained uniforms, attended regularly for drill, went on manoeuvres and knew they could be called up at any time. As was his style, Robert accepted all of this with charm and good humour. It did interfere with his life somewhat and he reflected that he had made a mistake in signing up for the Army rather than the Royal Air Force. Before National Service he had been an amateur pilot and was some way towards obtaining his licence. He preferred the style of the RAF as well as the prospect of flying for a living. With most young men, Robert did not imagine himself in a boiler suit, covered in grease, deep in the guts of an aeroplane but as a debonair pilot, smart in an almost fashionable uniform, adorned with glittering brocade. He would gladly have stayed on in the RAF.

The Reserves had the right to nominate members for Officer Training. Robert was clearly intelligent, university grade, well mannered and from the right background. Inevitably, the local commander thought him ideal material for a nomination and convinced Robert to allow his name to be put forward. At the end of an intensive officer training and assessment course, along with a dozen other candidates, he would be told whether or not he had been selected. During Robert's interview the reporting officer was very thorough in feeding back on every aspect of the course. Overall it was a positive report and before the end, Robert suspected that his life was about to take an unexpected turn and he would be spending the next long years as an officer in the Territorial Army. After some time, the reporting officer began to hedge. Finally, he apologised to Robert and told him that his application had been unsuccessful. Expecting this to be a considerable disappointment to the young man, the officer felt obliged to provide some explanation: 'Sorry, young man, but you're just too, well . . . womanish. Nothing personal, you understand. Your schooling is fine and you have the right qualifications. Apply next year and we'll see how it goes.'

Robert left the room and managed a smile. He had probably come close to a major error in his life. For the first time in a long while he thought of the Sergeant Major at Bodmin Moor, and the look which would cross his face had he chanced upon the women's clothes stowed carefully at the back of Robert's locker.

Sergeant Robert Pine did not apply for Officer Training again.

~

Dudley Teacher Training College, Birmingham, England. 1951. 'Universities are places of higher learning where those who do not require to support themselves go to continue their schooldays' was a common view in the 1950s. That the universities produced doctors, engineers, scientists and many other practitioners of useful contribution, seemed to some to be a happy accident or brought about by the brilliance or moral commitment of the individuals. Some of the older universities themselves were stuck in an earlier time and had problems admitting women, people of limited means or those who spoke with the wrong accent. In response to the social and economic needs of Britain in the middle of the twentieth century, colleges were formed. These colleges, while borrowing their generic title from the most ancient of educational establishments, were focused and pragmatic, being intent on producing individuals who could perform a job adequately. Robert Pine took himself to Dudley where teachers were produced under the auspices of Birmingham University. Mother's influence had won out again but Robert acknowledged to himself that even if he hated it he would still make good use of the long vacations.

Time out in the Army had served the purpose of convincing Robert that his aptitude for mathematics was almost as questionable as his liking for the subject. More and more he recognised his love of poetry, plays, music and painting. He wasted no time on regret but simply ensured that he trained as a teacher in Drama, Literature and Art. This was a good time in his life. National Service was gone for ever and he had done his bit. He viewed this as points scored or money in the bank towards his greater freedom. For three years he would lead an unstructured life compared to his lot in the Army and as a public schoolboy. Attending enough classes so as not to attract attention and trying just hard enough to pass each year and proceed, he would speed through college. Work was not a burden in that he was obliged to study all the subjects which fascinated the young man. As with students everywhere, the available extra-curricular activities were vast, and he participated in drama, singing and verse. To crown it all, when it came to an end he would be a teacher, earning a good salary for educating the young in the wonders of drama, literature and art for the rest of his days.

~

Loch Ard, Scotland. 1951.

Frank was a friend of Mother and Father so Robert thought of him as substantially older. How much older would have been difficult to identify as the young student moved through that period in his life when anyone over thirty years was simply old. Frank was on his own with no wife or obvious immediate family. Robert was not sure if Frank had been married and widowed or if he was a lifelong bachelor. Frank, he knew, was a seed merchant and obviously had a high standard of living. It was not polite to ask questions about his income and certainly not of your parents' friend. What was obvious was that Frank had a good income. He had his own home and a car. Not an old, many-owner, rattletrap such as Robert might aspire to but the latest saloon from Longbridge and changed just as often. Only a man of means could afford such a luxury.

The two men had a great deal in common in style and interests. In particular, they both shared a passion for Scotland and things Scottish. Robert had felt himself to be Scottish from an early age. If called on he could point to a couple of clues suggesting early influence such as the photograph of Father as a child, resplendent in kilt, or the book of Burns poetry bought for him as a child and cherished ever since. These clues were inadequate explanation for the depth of his feelings. While Frank loved the rugged and wild countryside that was Scotland, Robert actually felt Scottish. He therefore jumped at the offered opportunity to travel to the north on holiday with Frank.

The two men had been to Scotland numerous times and had become quite familiar with the routes and the terrain. Prior to each trip they would plot their itinerary and stop over at hotels, sharing rooms. Father and son travelling together was a common phenomenon and the hoteliers and bed and breakfast landladies are likely to have assumed that relationship between the two men. On this occasion they had run into difficulty in obtaining accommodation for the night and had been directed to a house by the banks of Loch Ard. They were given a room for the night but forewarned that there was a family christening. As the only guests, Frank and Robert were invited to join the family in the feast and celebration. From their initial difficulty, they now found themselves included in a party of traditional dimensions, hospitality and warmth. Toasts were made in the wetting of the baby's head. The tables pulled back, fiddle and accordion music filled the air and family members took turns to sing songs, some in the Gaelic. The whisky brought a heady pallor and the sweet, peaty aroma filled the air. The two men were accidental guests of honour and felt privileged as they realised that this large party of people were all family, apart from them, of course.

The grandfather called out for all to join the baby in the garden. Without protest or question the revellers traipsed out of the house led in procession by a piper. The swelling drones of the bagpipes reverberated in the hills and across the loch, music for open spaces both tuneful and evocative of that place in an earlier time. The garden carried all the way to the loch side and there the group gathered by a small hole, freshly dug through the turf. The baby was produced and the call was for her by name, 'Fiona Stewart Campbell'. In the fading light of the gloaming, a rowan tree was planted, for the luck of the child and to draw away the witches. Ruddy and warmed as much by the whisky as the tapping of his feet, Robert Pine stood and watched these people enact a ceremony of ancient rites and felt that he belonged.

~

Dudley Hippodrome, England. 1952.
People loved to be entertained and to watch others compete. Combine the two tastes and you have talent competitions. In 1950s Britain, every sizeable town ran such competitions, sometimes with significant prizes but more often attracting the contestants with the lure of being spotted by agents to take them to the big time. This aspect of British life contained a slice of the American dream where anyone can make it to the top regardless of their origins.

People had a great variety of guises to choose from and they all appeared: magicians doing card tricks, invisible from the auditorium; acrobats erecting ten-bodied pyramids; plate spinners using army surplus metal plates, destructible in the event of failure; stiff-chinned ventriloquists with beer-splattered wooden dummies; contortionists wrapping and chaining themselves in to glittering boxes; singing dogs looking cowed and humiliated, pink bows around their necks; synchronised pigeons walking tightropes on order for a seed reward and stopping to defecate on to the wood-splintered stage; ball-gowned opera singers trying too hard to reach that elusive note; dinner-suited pianists forgetting to smile at the audience as their fingers pounded the keys on an all-too-serious piece; comedians in loud-checked baggy suits and bashed fedoras, stealing each other's jokes; smooth-voiced crooners with greased hair and cigarettes; jugglers trying to catch that slippery sixth tennis ball or fourth Indian club; one-man bands all sounding the same, whatever tune they played; spoon players with a repertoire straight from drunken front-room parties; harmonica players sucking, blowing and dancing while aiming for a finale of speed and panache. Of course in show business they required some talent, a fact which many participants overlooked. Some audiences looked forward to the opportunity to berate and heckle the struggling acts, hoping that the performers would be forced to a stuttering collapse. Certain towns and halls were well known for their viciously unappreciative audiences. Dudley Hippodrome was a welcoming venue on the circuit and some acts appeared there just for the sake of performing.

The Lamplighters were an all-male singing group in the fashion of the time. They would sing almost any popular song in all sorts of styles but favoured that curious version of harmony popularised in the college boy films of Hollywood, Barber Shop. The Lamplighters sang and performed for pleasure. That is not to say they did not take the quality of the act seriously. They were all young students and gifted in their own way, writing and formatting their material and rehearsing regularly. They had the easy, careless attitude of the talented young who excelled at their hobby. They enjoyed singing for singing's sake as well as other artistic pursuits. Robert Pine was a member and, amongst other pursuits, belonged to three different dramatic groups, wrote poetry, drew and wrote for the college magazine. These activities were all over and above Robert's studies but he discerned no dividing line between work and play. They were equally important, pursued because they brought pleasure and, if artistic, required to be produced to the highest quality possible. The arts brought out in Robert the ability to work hard while feeling he was in pursuit of pleasure, not like mathematics at all. By the end of school, Robert was aware that mathematics was not for him and by the middle of college he wanted to pursue life as an actor. Life felt like an open adventure where with every step he refined and defined himself by discovery rather than by plan. Robert was a lucky man and he was enjoying himself.

One night, a London agent turned up at the Dudley Hippodrome intent on discovering amateur acts of potential and signing them for the music hall or working men's club circuits, the former on the wane while the latter waxed, soon to peak. The agent would sign the chosen act, arrange appearances, publicise them and hawk their talents to whoever was willing to pay. The payment to the performers would not be generous and depended on the number of bookings achieved. They would be obliged to go wherever they were booked to play and were likely to spend long years dragging cases full of outfits and props round the rainy, grimy industrial backwaters of England. They would stay in boarding houses run by fierce

landladies, serving fatty food and listing rules more pro-
hibitive than those of the harshest parent. Their personal
relationships would suffer as unpredictable income and
irregular contact took its toll. Most would work the circuit in
this manner for five, ten or twenty years, never progressing yet
refusing to give up till their health broke down, their thin
bookings disappeared or agents refused to have them as
clients. Yet this was the road to stardom in 1950s Britain and
every performer of every talent competition, every church
organist, every amateur player and every girl or boy crooning
songs to themselves in the privacy of their rooms – all dreamed
of being signed by an agent.

The Lamplighters performed well at Dudley Hippodrome
that night. The London agent had already heard of the singers
and paid them careful attention. After the show, the agent
turned up backstage and offered the group a professional
contract. They had made it out of the morass of hopeless
aspirants and all they had to do was sign. The seven young
men abandoned their occasional intellectual aloofness and
displayed their delight for once. They did not get carried away,
however, and asked for time to mull over the offer. Had they
been unemployed, shop assistants, labourers or in some other
occupation, paid a pittance and with no hope of advancement,
they would not have hesitated. But they were all students and
had other plans and a good future waiting for them. Under the
intoxicating glare of the spotlights most would have been
willing to change their life plans, desert their studies and sign
the contract. The one holding out, however, was a serious
scholar of merit and with firm work intentions after
university. He was also the Lamplighters' pianist and musical
virtuoso without whom they were nothing more than just
good singers. The contract was not signed, the Lamplighters
disbanded soon after and the members got on with their
studies and lives. Their lives differed from each other with that
inevitability of human separateness and idiosyncrasy. Had
they signed the contract, their paths might well have been
intrinsically linked for better or worse. It had been one of
those moments in the early flush of adulthood wherein a
choice of direction appears at a time when the recipients are
ill-equipped to appraise the options. The willing members of
the group did not see the contract as a major influence on their
lives but as a lark, a bit of a do that would be good for a

laugh. Of the group, Robert Pine suspected he was the most disappointed.

~

Venice, Italy. 1953.

The two men did not know that this would be their last holiday together. Robert had met Geoff Ash in the National Service, both having joined and left on the same day. Geoff had remained the only close friend since that time and they had spent several summers travelling over Europe. As students, albeit from reasonably comfortable homes, they were of limited means and opted for the cheapest possible mode of transport – other people's. Rambling, camping, walking and hitch-hiking were all seen as healthy pursuits, to be pursued by anyone and not exclusive to the young or impoverished. The car had come into its own since the end of the War as had the transportation of goods by lorry. This, aligned with the socially acceptable face of hitch-hiking, opened to people vistas previously well out of reach. Robert and Geoff, Pine and Ash, took full advantage of the free lifts.

In the Army the two men had been ribbed about their surnames and this may have been a happy accident, causing them to speak and discover a great deal in common. They had gone their separate ways after the enforced service but wrote and took these holidays. That morning they had travelled into Venice for the first time. Entranced by its cragged, damp beauty they had walked around, sightseeing by touch and guesswork. This had led to a few wrong turnings, discovering themselves in an alleyway, three feet broad, wedged between buildings, face-to-face with a wall. They retired to an open-air café to recover and quench a growing thirst and ended up reminiscing about their times abroad.

France was the target for the first venture, being closest and having a language in which Ash and Pine reckoned they had passable expertise. They had mixed blessings on the hitch-hiking front with some remarkable lifts to recall – like the French version of the Austin A7, unrecognisable to the two Englishmen and appearing as a heap of rusting metal bolted together from the outside. Six or seven priests already packed the small car, so crowded the driver had to lean to one side with his head out of the window, steering with one hand. Christian charity prevailed and the recipients, Ash and Pine, sped through the glorious French countryside, perched on the running boards at either side of the car. France had been unable to invest heavily on road repairs over the previous ten years and the sudden bumps and jolts of gaping potholes threatened to send the tourists spilling in to deep, slime-coated ditches.

The French welcome to the pair was recalled as warm, almost grateful. The people of the villages had lived through a war in their very back yard and the Liberation was recent history of the utmost importance. It was a good time to be British and visiting France. The young men could not muster much of a contribution to the war effort between them but happily accepted gratitude in villages, towns, bars and roadsides all over the country. The benefits were manifold and only some were recalled that day.

Like the couple who picked them up in a Citroën 2CV, a car which even then looked homemade or designed cheaply for the poorest of families: they had insisted on taking the men to their house which turned out to be a grand château in the mountains. Later that night the hospitality had extended to unlimited wine at a dance in the local village. From a French dance hall, thoughts turned to a Spanish dance arena where Ash and Pine watched a fireworks display with new eyes. In the warm breeze of the evening, a rocket lost its way and set off horizontally through the sky, dipping into the open-air café and scoring a bull's eye on the pate of a rotund, shiny-headed customer. The target was distressed but the onlookers were in tears of laughter.

Memories of a walk through the night from Spain and over the Pyrenees to arrive in France as dawn broke, of the first trip to Spain where trouble still rumbled under the dictatorship of General Franco and the military evident everywhere. Walking down a dusty road, smelling the magnolia and heading to the border, they were ambushed by armed soldiers pointing loaded rifles and speaking in a rapid, lisping Spanish, inaccessible to the frightened young men. Passports displayed and on their way, Ash and Pine ended the day watching the sunset in Spain and catching the sunrise in France.

A time in France when the mundane difficulties of those shared events, miserable at the time, funny at a later date, bound the participants together. Failing to get a lift for hours in the rain, the two agreed to separate, go in different directions but to meet at their proposed destination. First off was Geoff, speeding away in the sheltered comfort of a car. An hour later, Robert finally got a lift on the back of a motorbike, a common form of transport. Swishing through the warm drizzle, in a short while they came to a crossroads. The biker, with an apologetic shrug, deposited Robert by the roadside and sped off on his way. Robert stood by that road now drenched through, feeling sorry for himself, not a common occurrence. In a short while a car drew up and the door swung open. Skipping gratefully to take up the lift, Robert paused at the open door to be greeted by his friend and travelling companion. Having set off in different directions at different times and on different routes, the friends could not ascertain how they had come to be at the same point on this road. No doubt they knew that the explanation was readily available to those more familiar with the road systems. They preferred to remember it as a little bit of magic.

Now it was 1953 and they were in Venice, a place of charm, colour and atmosphere. Robert could imagine the days of the empire and the wars between cities. He felt the history and was moved to recall Scotland, lochs, bagpipes and a baby called Fiona Stewart Campbell. Venice and Scotland had for him the same type of feeling, a sense of knowing the past while living in the present.

The two young tourists journeyed out to Isola della Giudecca for the practical purpose of staying overnight in the modern convenience of a youth hostel. Having found the place and dumped their rucksacks, they noticed a poster advertising a performance of *Twelfth Night* nearby. Late in the evening, under the clearest, blackest sky providing a backcloth for stars somehow stronger, brighter and more numerous than back home in England, the two young men watched and listened to Shakespeare as never before. Geoff tried hard to follow the script as the actors deployed their native Italian. Robert watched the movement and marvelled at the startling colours of the costumes and the shifting rustle of the dresses. He had the feeling that this was how Shakespeare intended the play, even if the language was not his English. The cast were all male, as in the original, and Robert moved between an envy of those in dresses and an appreciation of the production's strength. Later, the two friends chatted about the play over a nightcap, sipped at a table in the open air in a piazza still humming with the movement of people. Robert shared with his friend his view that the characters were more complete, being acted by men. Geoff debated the issue and acknowledged that while he could not entirely agree, he understood what Robert meant. In future years, Geoff Ash would be asked to understand his friend again. He may have looked back at that hot night by the canals of Venice, when he and his friend discussed men wearing dresses.

~

Birmingham, England. 1954.

Adulthood starts for some with their marriage, their own home, the first job which allow the financial and personal freedom to make their own decisions and mistakes. Robert Pine did not see life in such a rigid manner, life for him being a continuum of opportunity and discovery. Starting work as a teacher did mark some kind of watershed. He could remember from the age of twelve having a view of what he wanted from adult life. Although many of his views had changed since then he still aspired to good money, long holidays and being paid for helping others to discover the wonders of the arts in every shade and nuance. He had arrived in the sense that he was now a teacher, his parents were proud and he had already made his way in the world. He intended to make his way some more.

Mother and Father were feeling very satisfied with themselves, seeing how their two children had turned out. Both well educated, good looking, popular among their friends, talented in different ways, teachers with good prospects of careers and marriage. Father's life was much the same as it had always been only more so with greater time being spent on his art projects, reading and scrapbooks. His aptitudes had a new focus and one very close to his heart, Eva. Mother had become a Councillor for the Conservative Party and was fast achieving a position of prominence. She was regularly obliged to give speeches, open fêtes or chair meetings. These occasions were mainly for the Council but also involved the NSPCC and her adopted charity. Mother was increasingly out and about of evenings and weekends, leaving Father at home with his projects. Father's main outside interests included the occasional visit to church on Sunday and frequent attendance at the Masonic Lodge. He was a committed Freemason and had worked himself up to high office, first locally then nationally. Father encouraged Robert to join the Lodge but the son refused to show any interest. Father and son had so much in common but the church and the Freemasons were to remain the exceptions.

Most nights Father could be found working on the hard table by the fire. He was a gifted wordsmith and had worked at this for most of his life. Thus, he happily fell into preparing and writing many of his wife's speeches. She had the energy, commitment and social skills while Father had the sensitivity and touch for the spoken word. It often seemed to Robert that his father did most of the work and his mother would pick up on his labours and take all the credit. This never occurred to William Pine as he pursued another favourite pastime of scrapbooks, many of which were now dedicated to the speeches and public appearances of his wife, his Eva.

Tina was doing so well in her parents' eyes with her post of teacher settled and a growing intimacy between her and one or two beaux including Geoff Ash, or so they hoped. They had come to know Geoff through Robert and he had appeared fond of their daughter. Robert suspected his parents of strong encouragement, just falling short of matchmaking. Geoff was a capable and cultured young man who would do well for himself. Tina was full of spunk and energy. She was likely to go shooting off abroad on a whim and always more likely to do that than sit at home darning the socks. She had vitality enough for two and it would take someone special to keep up with her. William and Eva thought Geoff was special.

Robert had started his teaching career and his parents believed this would be the making of him and no mistake. They had been quietly pleased about how he had bitten the bullet and got on with his National Service with no complaints. Both were openly proud of each of his promotions in the Army and making Sergeant was damn good, they thought. While he clearly detested the drudgery of hard work, he had made his way through college and still found time to join in every club or drama society. Father suspected that Robert really wanted to be an actor and was relieved his son had made that a pastime while he had actually become a teacher. Both had a sense of relief that those habits of Robert's when a child, that dressing-up business had found an acceptable outlet. They had been worried then but understood it now as his inclination towards performing, towards acting. Mother and Father did not talk about those worrying early days in Robert's life – not to each other and never to their son.

Robert started at the school with his usual expectancy of new experiences and happy outcomes. The school was in the inner circle of Birmingham, then a vast morass of building sites squeezed between slums and dereliction. The War had knocked the stuffing out of the city and it was being rebuilt. First priority in this process of rebirth was a replacement of the industrial base, vital to get the stuttering economy of the country back on its feet, provide jobs for the vast workforce and provide incomes to some of the poorest families in Europe. Next priority was housing. Some way down the list came schools.

The threshold of Robert's teaching career was to be on the upper floor of a red-brick Victorian building in a deprived area of Smethwick. Robert was to find out that his class of thirty was made up of young children with learning disabilities, emotional damage, disturbed behaviour. Some came from impoverished homes and struggled to get enough food or find warm, weather-proof clothing, their families from that area of human misery where alcoholism, prostitution, child abuse, neglect, incest and desertion all played a part. Many lived with one parent, the War leaving widows or life taking its toll in the more routine way of marital breakdown. Robert felt he had been pitched in beyond his depth. These children deserved all the help they could get and he would try his best in spite of the obstacles of their circumstances and their struggle just to survive in life. However, without the specialist training for this work he was soon to realise he would be unequal to the challenge and sought a move to another school.

On the first day of his second year, Robert was introduced to his class in a long, wood-framed school hall, the same room where assembly was held. He was there to teach an entire curriculum, not just the Crafts and Arts he had trained for, but he assumed there would be obvious benefits from the space afforded by the location. He was to be disillusioned very quickly when a crocodile column of children came marching into the room, taking up their seats at the far end of the hall all the while shouting, whistling and slapping each other. Thinking there was some mistake he approached the ruddy-faced man in a sports jacket, carrying a pile of blue-covered jotters and walking behind the interlopers. In clipped tones the man advised him that this was his class and his classroom. The new young teacher took an age to understand but eventually did with a sense of disbelief. He was to teach fifty children in the same room as someone else teaching another fifty children with only a curtain between them.

'Well,' thought Robert, 'this will be an adventure.'

~

Birmingham, England. 1956.

It was Robert's last day at school and his last day ever as a teacher of Crafts and Arts to children. He had endured a career which could be calculated in months and spanned two schools. He was an angry and bitter young man. Those who knew the work he was required to do would assume that the intransigence and backwardness of his pupils had driven him to leave. Most would sympathise with him rather than the children, believing they were not worthy. While that time was full of social reform with free health care, education for all, nationalisation and the promise of full employment, attitudes were a harder burden to shift. The poor, the damaged and the disturbed were on the edges of society, placed there by people. These children were at the centre of Robert's concern and he felt they deserved all that could be provided. The children had not driven him from teaching, though they were certainly difficult to teach. Teachers had driven him from teaching.

When the nineteen-year-old Robert Pine had volunteered for the Army Education Corps he had no way of knowing his contribution would come back to haunt him so soon. The day had come when he realised that many of his teaching colleagues were ex-Army people, utilising their newly certificated status to enter the profession. Robert had understood that this might happen. What he had no way of predicting was the extent of apathy aligned with discipline based on punishment alone and meted out by many of his colleagues. The educational facilities were lacking, the space was vastly overcrowded and the needs of the children were unquenchable but he still believed that schooling could be provided, given the commitment of the staff. Robert had changed schools, suspecting he had drawn a bad bunch on his first placement, only to find a worsening situation. He found himself detesting the thought of work and feeling angry with his colleagues before anything happened. Time and again he watched the level of trust and understanding he had worked to cultivate in a particular child ruined by one bad-tempered, careless colleague.

Robert Pine was twenty-five years old and left jaundiced by a system which met the responsibility of teaching future generations by formula or rote rather than by meeting human needs. In the last short while he had discovered many things about other people and about himself. Those who claimed to be professional, dedicated and in control sometimes obscured a lack of interest by a gruff manner, delivering the right jargon in a precise, business-like style. That is, they were in disguise and more ambitious for self than for the others they served. Of himself he had learned that he could care for others even while he cared for himself. The easy-going, artistic liberal that he was discovered he had standards which were not a universal affliction. The young Robert thought he was tainted and weakened by his standards though later he would recognise a blessing.

Robert Pine left teaching after thirty-six months. They had felt like the longest thirty-six months of his life to date. Decades later he could not think of those months without feeling fury at teachers who simply did not care for or listen to the children they taught.

9 Marriage, Children and Commercial Enterprise

Happiness in marriage is entirely a matter of chance.
JANE AUSTEN IN 'PRIDE AND PREJUDICE'

Birmingham, England. 1956.
Depending on who asked him, Robert Pine might describe his career change as moving from education to industry or, perhaps, from teaching to the sale of sandpaper. He now worked for Minnesota Mining & Manufacturing Co., had started in the office as a management recruit and benefited from their policy of moving staff around to gain experience of the whole company. The mid-1950s witnessed an increase in the study of people in organisations, led by America of course. Those were exciting times for social psychologists and sociologists, exploring every dimension of human behaviour, unhindered by any established body of knowledge.

Robert found himself easily bored by the office routine and discovered a predilection for selling. Getting out and about, meeting people, coming across as genuine, trustworthy and convincing were activities he enjoyed. When necessary he would deploy tricks from his acting repertoire and maintain a charming front against all the odds – not to deceive but, when antagonised, to shield the conversation from a downward, disintegrating spiral. He was good at selling and commission rates rewarded success. From this beginning, Robert soon found himself with a good salary, self-respect, a car, travel throughout the Midlands and the north of England, all within working hours sufficiently civilised to allow full rein to his other interests which he pursued with vigour.

At school he had discovered particular pleasure in all racquet games and much preferred tennis to sweaty, bruising rugby or staid, stiff-lipped cricket. Some may assume that the young

Robert had been avoiding the danger of team sports but this was to misunderstand him entirely. At King Edward's School he played a game called fives, a sort of deadly squash. The court was outside and open at the top and rear. The walls were made of rough concrete against which enthusiastic players would scrape their knuckles or, swinging their arms in too wide an arc, crumple their limbs, splintering their wrists or breaking their arms. At the side of the court there was a concrete obstacle at shoulder height, some three yards from the front wall, and a deep step ran straight across it to the opposite side. Fives was played with a large, thick-skinned glove and a hard ball with a dull bounce. The game required energy, strength, balance and a great deal of courage. It surprised no one that fives was not a popular game, that is, outwith the older public schools. King Edward's played fives in competition with Harrow, Eton and all the major schools, the only establishments in England to bother building the right courts. Played well and with determination, fives made rugby look like a soft option. Robert Pine played fives.

As an adult, Robert discovered badminton and quickly achieved a certain level of competence. Aligned with his regular attendance, this skill led him to fill a position of rising prominence among local badminton players. He was a young man, tall, slim, suave, energetic, intelligent, cultured, with a good salary and quality of life. All these factors made for an attractive potential partner in the mating rituals. His skill in the sport was also important since everyone may love a loser, but they prefer to be on the side of a winner.

The 1950s middle-class view allowed a man to postpone settling down for a period during which he was expected to experience life, establish himself in gainful employment or otherwise achieve an income to support self, wife and children. A woman was permitted a period of grace but shorter in duration and with some clear, limited perspective on what experiences of life were acceptable for her to pursue. A man may 'sow his wild oats' but woe betide any woman caught in such debauchery. For a woman, regardless of her personal attributes, if she was still unmarried beyond a certain age, questions were asked of her worth. Failing to make a match during young adulthood would result in the most derogatory labelling of women. They were left on the shelf, old maids, of low morality or in possession of objectionable personality traits. It was assumed that all women were heterosexual, destined for maternity and incomplete without a legal bond to a man. Of a man drifting into his thirties and forties without a hint of matrimony, some questions might be asked. Socially, the most damaging conclusions would imply homosexuality, closely followed by the description of being a mummy's boy, while the safest allowed for the status of confirmed bachelor. A confirmed bachelor was deemed to have chosen to remain unmarried, all the better to pursue unhindered masculine activities like sport, hunting, travel, cigar smoking and drinking strong liquor. The longer this state of confirmed singularity continued, the less attractive a matrimonial prospect the fellow became, having developed his own habits and routines which would prove difficult to convert to the necessary compromises of a partnership. All in all, by far the easiest route was to do the right and expected thing by getting married to someone of good character and to do so within the accepted age band, not too early and not too late.

Robert was twenty-five years old and would soon be twenty-six. He thought it was time to do the right thing and get married, so he started to look about at the women of his acquaintance. He had many friends through his numerous pastimes and quickly came to the view that Doreen Keeling, a badminton enthusiast, would make the best match. The young woman was attractive, bright, obviously fit and healthy. Doreen was twenty-nine years old and ready for marriage. She came from Dudley, was part of a family of five strong sisters and was close to them all, but one sister in particular. Robert and Doreen saw a great deal of each other simply by their independent pursuit of badminton and knew they had that much in common before they started courting. Their relationship blossomed with only a little adjustment to their lifestyles and their commitment to the racquet game was enhanced by the romance. Robert had many other interests in amateur dramatics, drawing, poetry and many more. Doreen's hobby was badminton and badminton alone.

Robert and Doreen were married on 13 October 1956.

~

Dudley, Midlands, England. 1957.
Marriage suited Robert. Doreen was a careful and supportive partner who did not interfere with his life as it had been before the wedding. The newly-weds had reached an arrangement with Doreen's sister Margaret and her soon-to-be husband, Alan Fabb. The two couples brought their resources together and

bought a house jointly. Robert and Doreen moved into the house right away and were to be joined by the Fabbs once they were married. The 1950s were financially stringent times and the rental house market had yet to fully recover from the damage of the War. While the Pines and the Fabbs were doing well they were at the start of their earning potential and would find it difficult to find and afford good-quality accommodation on their own. Together they bought a fine home which served them well for the first years of married life. Families pooling resources and sharing homes were not unusual. Margaret and Alan Fabb did not live in the house until after their marriage. While they had invested money in a house they did not occupy, they would have the benefit of having a fully furnished home to move into immediately after their wedding, an unusually good start for young couples at that time. The Pines would set the home up and would eventually share it with the Fabbs. They had the advantage of a good-quality home which would otherwise be beyond their means. That and the house to themselves for the initial period, a greatly privileged position for a young married couple at that time.

Robert and Doreen, as with all newly-married couples, found themselves playing at 'houses' for real. Their domestic arrangements now centred on each other and their own home. Otherwise, Robert continued more or less as before with the most obvious change being a sharper realisation of the need to earn more money. He had now moved on to a company called Kalamazoo and was travelling throughout the Midlands of England selling their products, a range of stationery, office equipment and administrative systems. This style of work suited Robert better than the more practical and industrial range of the Minnesota Co. Kalamazoo was, by contrast, a thoroughly British organisation and Robert prospered in the entrepreneurial environment created by this market leader.

It was the age of the advent of the travelling salesman and tens of thousands of men moved up and down the country flogging their wares. The term 'travelling salesman' was generic and included: the man in a raincoat standing on doorsteps with a bashed suitcase full of brushes; the man with the back seat of his car full of women's and children's clothing, claiming they were the latest fashions at the lowest prices; men in little Ford vans, cold-canvassing corner shops, touting the sale of large jars of peppermint-flavoured pan drops, tart-tasting pineapple chunks or sweet-smelling parma violets. The breed sold almost everything including paint, encyclopaedias, fruit, vegetables, scissors, life insurance, sponges, detergents, saving plans, washing machines and so on. Many of the goods could be purchased on credit, phased at unexplained interest rates and lasting for ever and a day. The majority of salesmen were paid on commission only and received an extra cut for setting up credit arrangements. The poorest people were often targeted and the salesman forced to lose all scruples to earn a wage by convincing potential customers they could afford items well beyond their pocket by paying on the never-never. Commercial salesmen earned a bad reputation.

Robert Pine was not that type of commercial salesman. Selling to companies only, he dealt in larger sums of money and negotiated with managers, wise to the ways of commerce. Often he was involved in helping his customers solve problems of record keeping, information storage or statistical analysis, as Kalamazoo specialised in manual systems addressing such requirements. He had found a job which he enjoyed, brought in good money, challenged his intellect now and then while never sapping his creative energy, allowing him a deal of freedom.

Life seemed to be the success Robert had planned, albeit making an adjustment or two along the way. A young, attractive wife, a home of their own, good salaries and plenty of time for his drama, poetry, literature and badminton. She did not share most of these pastimes with her husband. Doreen did not mind any of Robert's pursuits but did not participate herself apart, that is, from the badminton.

~

Dudley, Midlands, England. 1959.
Selling was stressful on the individual for a number of reasons and many people could not cope with some of the demands. Compared with an office job, the hours were uncertain, irregular and frequently carried on well past the six o'clock deadline. Robert enjoyed the independence of this dimension to the post. While driven by the expectations of customers in reality, he felt a little more control when negotiating the time of meetings or visits. As long as he kept selling enough goods, the company were not too concerned about how or when he worked. Robert hated early mornings and found that he could

not avoid such dawn rises as often as he wished. Still, he would sometimes struggle out of bed, shave, get into his suit and after a hurried cup of tea rush away to his first meeting only to discover a gap in his diary later. Occasionally, he considered such a gap to be earned free time.

Driving in to his neat cul-de-sac, he nodded at some neighbours going about their domestic business – scrubbing front doorsteps, washing windows, walking back from the corner grocers, shopping bags heavy with the daily groceries. The neighbours were not surprised to see Bob Pine at home during the day, being familiar with his job and accustomed to his sporadic daytime appearances. Doreen, Margaret and Alan were at work and he knew exactly when they would return. Parking his car by the kerb directly in front of his house, he extracted his briefcase and a small package from the boot. Robert looked tall and elegant in his tailored suit, holding himself erect and walking with a crisp, confident manner. Any neighbour sneaking a glance through shifting net curtains would observe the very essence of a young businessman of executive stature: 'Nothing to worry about there. Not like her at the end . . . Nice couple, Bob and Doreen Pine – good sorts, reliable and so close.' Or so the peeking neighbour thought.

Robert Pine watched himself in the mirror as he pulled on the dress. He managed to wear some of Doreen's clothes but not enough due to the size difference and had to buy his own to ensure a reasonable fit. He was now almost at ease with his trips to female lingerie and outfit stores, knowing his sizes and purchasing his goods in towns well away from home where no one knew him or his wife. He considered these trips as some of the unforeseen bonuses of the job as was the opportunity to slip home during the day. Robert was of the view that he was a lucky man, always discovering little plus points where previously there had been seemingly insurmountable obstacles.

At first he had felt constricted by the confines of his marriage. He had known Doreen as a girlfriend and fiancée and believed he was familiar with all her ways. Learning to live together was entirely different and a greater strain than he had anticipated. As a general point, he considered that the social mores should be altered to oblige engaged couples to live together for a period prior to taking their vows. Robert was not in favour of a loosening of moral standards but thought it a sensible precaution for couples intending to stay together for the remainder of their lives, to discover at least if they could live together for a few months. Both he and, he suspected, Doreen had to discover aspects of each other not readily on display in public and certainly not at the badminton club. Habits, routines, preferences for sleeping on a particular side of the bed, marmalade or honey on the breakfast toast, starch or none in the washing, dinner immediately after work or later, time needed in the toilet, mood on first awakening? The list of small questions added up to one big statement: on the day they were married they did not know each other very well at all.

The new Mr and Mrs Pine had survived and adjusted over the first few months, settling down to the comfort of an established relationship. Robert adjusted the hem of his dress and asked himself what Doreen would think if she could see him now. He did not allow the question to worry him too often since he was convinced that his wife could not cope with his habit. Doreen would think he had gone mad. She was a conservative person with firm opinions on right and wrong only vouchsafed when provoked. In the main, she wanted to go on through life with as little upset or unusual happenings as possible.

Robert's need to dress in women's clothes was deeply personal and, he thought, unique. He alone had this need and so others would struggle to comprehend, as he himself struggled. Doreen would have a sense of men wanting to be with men and women wanting to be with women, or so he suspected, not having discussed such behaviour with his wife. He was equally convinced she would treat such sexual preferences as wrong and, therefore, beyond any further discussion. Robert anticipated Doreen's view of a man in a skirt as homosexual, mad or both. Could she actually comprehend her husband, happy with his marriage and his lot in life, simply needing to dress in women's clothing from time to time? Not in a million years.

The net curtain billowed slightly as if by a breeze. The old woman in the neighbouring house bent at her window and observed that nice gentleman Bob Pine march sprightly down his path, briefcase in one hand, package under the same arm. 'Such a fine upstanding young man,' she thought. 'Nice couple. A credit to the street and no doubt.'

Robert Pine placed his burdens in the car boot then locked it with the key, twisting the chrome-plated device to determine it was secure. He stood for a moment, staring at his home, aware that he himself was probably being observed by one or two neighbours. Looking at the house, for the umpteenth time he checked over in his mind the order and precision he had deployed in ensuring that he had tidied away any incriminating evidence. Unlocking the car boot, he checked his package and counted the items of clothing. Finally convinced that he had covered his tracks, he sat in the car and drove away to his next assignment, at peace with the world and alone with his secret.

~

Glasgow, Scotland. 1965.

Parenthood had brought such happiness for Robert Pine. He counted the birth of his two children as the two most profound effects on his life to date. As a newly-married man, he had assumed that children would come along but had not con-templated the prospect in much more detail. It was just something that would happen and he would learn how to deal with it when necessary. He was not prepared for the sense of responsibility, belonging and meaning which had emerged from their births. It was as if a new Robert had emerged into the world with the babies and their crying, grumpy little wrinkled faces. He had not been present at the births – it was not the done thing – but he often wished he had been there to see if they brought with them a special glowing beam, message or some other signal. Such thoughts were fanciful nonsense, he realised, but such was his surprise at the impact of his children on him that he imagined they had brought some magic spell, changing him for ever. The old him had gone and his children would never know that other Robert Pine. Their father was a different person from the man who married their mother, went to school, worked as a teacher, and hitch-hiked in France. He found himself wanting to say 'thank you' to his two children: 'Thank you for giving me a gift I had never before imagined.'

Fiona and Duncan had practical effects on their father as well. For example, he was now determined to make as much money as possible and promptly stopped playing at the business of selling. He had not seen himself as less than serious at work before but now the urgency to take home enough money to provide adequately for his children was acute. No more dodging back home if there was a space in his diary. If such a gap appeared, he promptly filled it with some prospect of a sale, no matter how slim. His work carried him farther afield now, the length and breadth of the country. Time to reflect on happy days at home when he would pick his way through the chaos that is a house first thing in the morning, with one infant and a baby, take some time over the children and out the door, a man with a mission.

Robert had always been poor at remembering dates. Not 1066 and all that, but anniversaries, birthdays, the year he started school or joined the Army. His mind did not work that way in that, of any event, he recalled feelings, views, fragrances and faces with unerring accuracy but did not seem to have room to locate the happening on the calendar. He could not recall the day of his wedding – not the day of the week, the month, the year even. The blind spot did not mean that he cared less for Doreen, his mind simply did not work that way. However, he knew the dates of birth of both his children: Fiona, born on 21 September 1960; Duncan, born on 18 April 1964. The dates were in his mind, sometimes slipping into his consciousness when not intended, like checking his diary for the working months ahead or while watching a young woman push a pram down the pavement. The dates were a simple symbol of how he felt his children had changed him for ever.

~

Leeds, England. 1971.

Computers – great, bulky tanks of memory storage and keyboards which required precise, coded instruction were already on sale by the late 1960s. The advances they offered were evident to many and the public were beginning to develop some vague notion of their potential. Large-scale industries, colleges, universities, government offices, the police, the Armed Forces and research institutes were investing in computers and Robert Pine was selling them. He worked for a company called Frieden, at the time a leading company in the field of what was about to be called new technology.

The move from Kalamazoo made sense since the manual systems they had developed were being replaced by computers and much more besides. Living and working in the north of England, Robert was also dealing with many of his previous customers. He had a well established reputation as an excellent company representative, as someone who never failed to make targets or meet quotas of sales. In his working life, Robert had become a specialist at selling to companies. His high professional standards had served him well as he prospered through the 'never had it so good' contention of the Macmillan Government and he would survive the wage freeze being imposed by Prime Minister Harold Wilson.

Fiona and Duncan were fit and healthy children who would grow to be assertive and intelligent adults. Their father had been inducted to the worries of a parent, that almost paranoid dimension wherein the paramount belief is that anything can go wrong at any time. While Robert recognised those feelings as a gnawing ache, placed somewhere just under the skin of his upper stomach, he remained the optimist for whom life had gone well so far with no apparent reason for this to change. Doreen was coping with the primary role of parent and saw to it that he was allowed to concentrate on his work and his pastimes.

Elsewhere life had moved on apace. For some people the 1960s had meant the space race, a man going to the moon, the Beatles, flower power, war in Vietnam. For Robert it meant parenthood, his mother becoming the Conservative Mayor of Oldbury and awarded the MBE for her charitable activities, his father's untimely death; all these other things and April Ashley. Always an avid reader of the newspapers, Robert had noticed a slow dribble of reports about men who wanted to be women. The revelation hit him like a sledge hammer blow. Robert, along with much of the British population, had not conceived that such a change would be possible. The newspapers suggested that operations had been carried out in some countries. Robert dismissed the reports due to their salacious style, the journalists concentrating on the sex angle. Anyway, he was interested only as any member of the public would be interested.

There was no personal significance of these reports on sex changes for Robert, it was that straightforward. He was amazed at the speed of scientific and medical breakthrough, aligned with social upheaval. People seemed determined to challenge and push the terms of their existence to the extremes. No longer would they accept deprivation, powerlessness and restriction as their lot in life. The pursuit of personal freedom and liberty was becoming like a secular religion in a church of zealots. When Robert thought about the rate of change in the world it almost made him giddy. Heart transplants, women's liberation, contraceptive pills, walking in space, serial killers on Saddleworth Moor, Churchill dead, cannabis, the assassination of presidents, Florence flooded and a Cultural Revolution in China used as an excuse to berate and exterminate people. All that, and now the prospect of people being able to choose to change sex. Exciting, unsettling times.

Robert Pine found himself with an increasing collection of newspaper clippings – first folded and slipped between the back pages of a diary like Father's scraps, waiting to be more carefully placed on the broad pages of a book. All Robert's scraps were about sex changes.

10 Fear and Anger

Anger is a brief madness.
HORACE IN 'EPISTLES' CIRCA 65BC–8BC

It was a Sunday evening, an unusual day and time for Newman to be travelling to Tarbert. Her working week had stretched to include a conference in Brighton spanning over into the weekend. Newman detested such events where vainglorious speaker after vainglorious speaker strutted their stuff, trying too hard to be more radical than the last. Now she could pick and choose the lectures she attended, thank God, unlike when she started in the business and had to be seen at everything, or so her sponsors advised. It had been less of a burden then since it was all new and she was determined to succeed. It did not feel easy at the time though she was aware that many talented, dedicated people would wait years for a breakthrough. Newman's early effort attracted the support of a major company and she had achieved a minor success with her first published work. She was only too aware that, even then, it could all end in tears. One promising start did not make a reputation other than for one promising start and she had a long way to travel.

In the early days, Newman had been enthralled just to be invited to these weekend extravaganzas. Half the people present were her heroes or, at the very least, people she admired even if she was none too keen on their style. For most, simply getting there was a monumental struggle, hard work, long hours, constant rejection and revision with a peppering of luck and a soupçon of good timing. These people had been at the top for years and that took staying power. The other half of the attendance list were administrators, managers, commissioners who would, she knew, wield a greater influence on her success or failure in the long run. For the first few years she had to pander to their every whim and did so by going to every event, every publicity shoot, every cheese and wine shindig and every launch, throughout it all being as sociable and friendly as she could muster. There was no casting couch in this business. Well, none she had *discovered*.

'How far was I willing to go back then? Exactly what were my personal limits? Did I have any limits at all?' were questions she asked herself when she had grown bored with it all, a more and more common state these days. Thinking back twenty-odd years she could only remember the work she produced and her overriding enthusiasm to be in print. Trouble was, she was remembering through the weary, cynical, seen-it-all-twice attitudes she had now. The person she had become sometimes suspected that the younger Newman would have done anything while, at other times, she suspected that the younger Newman would have died on the spot. Then again, she wondered if she had changed at all.

The Sunday evening felt like a Sunday evening, as if the fizz had escaped, leaving a lukewarm, saccharine dribble flopping around at the bottom of the bottle. She recalled a childhood conundrum about the seven days of the week, when did it begin and when did it end. The childish banter went on in terms of Sundays being days of rest but did you do this after work, before work or was there any difference? She could tell those children to hold their fire till they reached a certain age and, on the same day: stay up most of the night drinking gin and listening to inane banter; snatch two hours' sleep in a stuffy hotel bedroom; wake up with a start and a headache; catch a slow service train and spend the journey wondering where the overwhelming smell of cats was coming from; sit in Heathrow for three hours waiting for an aeroplane, broken down on the runway, within your field of vision; board a flight to Glasgow and let turbulence reawaken your hangover; realise you cannot remember where you parked your car; run out of paracetamol; find your car parked as far from the terminal as is possible; then head west and drive through fast failing light on the roads of Argyll. Newman had had a bad day but it provided the insight that Sundays were the dog-end of the week.

Newman's headache was lifting as the light was falling. She watched the waters of the loch change from murky grey to pitch and admitted to herself that she found the area beautiful in the bleakest of weather and the blackest of nights. She had grown comfortable with handling her car on the treacherous bends and dips of the road but still the aura of Argyll tempted her concentration off and into a waking dream. She had observed this scene when the night was so dark no shapes were visible, the curves of the hills and shores of the waters smothered by a blanket, dense and black. She had watched sheep move around the hills after midnight, deceived that day prevailed by the light of the moon. She had gasped at a moon so large and red, bringing on fancies of burnt-out suns and blistered planets. Then there were the Sunday nights with nothing out of the ordinary, just the glory of the Highlands closing down for the day.

Nature's display pulled Newman's mind to leave behind the trivia of the last few days and feel a part of the world she was entering. She thought of the Cottage waiting for her and was grateful for her discipline in collecting wood for the stove on her last visit. She looked forward to a late supper and music, some symphony to soothe the last taste of the city out of her system. A stroll down the rough-hewn sheep path to the loch side and along the banks a short way, serenaded by the lapping of the water and the anguished call of birds, prehistoric in their tone, a mystery to their lone audience. She longed to turn and look back at the winking lights from the Cottage windows, feeling the stove's heat and the welcome of familiar objects. Back up the path with heather branches brushing her coat, her essence breeze-cooled and refreshed.

Newman also wondered about the others in that community, what they would be doing as the day came to a close. Later, as she supped a brandy nightcap, she would work through her character list, inventing activities for them all based on a little prior knowledge, like a scriptwriter deciding on the soap opera's next sensation. As she drove, her thoughts turned to Robert and Jean Pine, as they always did when she thought of the people of Tarbert. She carried out a mental calculation and reckoned that by then, 1987, they had been in Tarbert for five years. Rumours hinted that the Pines were considering the sale of Springside Cottage, giving up the bed and breakfast, and buying Ashens Cottage. Ashens was a mile or two outside Tarbert, close to the driveway entrance to Stonefield Castle Hotel. The cottage was on its own by the side of the main road leading into and down the peninsula of Kintyre. As with all the other drivers, Newman frequently passed Ashens Cottage which looked as if it needed some repairs and upgrading – always difficult and slow in

Argyll. Newman shivered at the memory of the nightmare of her own efforts at the Cottage and felt a twinge of sympathy for the Pines. Just an iota of concern, since Robert and Jean were doing well by all accounts. Robert's shop, Kiltie's, was a purveyor of goods to visiting yacht people and the sole provider of newspapers and other items on a Sunday. Jean was to work full time at the Columba Hotel and had built a growing reputation for tasty fare. Neither of these developments were what the Pines had planned, but it was typical of Bob Pine to be lucky.

Newman suspected the move to Ashens Cottage would be more threatening for the Pines for reasons other than the scale of maintenance and repairs. The couple would be moving out of the village. Were they well enough established to maintain their good standing? What if something went wrong in the future, would the villagers still stand by the Pines? Newman sensed that Bob Pine was about to break his luck and smiled to herself as she watched a long-winged bird of prey sweep high over the banks of the loch to plummet down, snatching and crushing some unseen, unsuspecting victim.

Behind Newman's car, a convoy had developed. Her scenic ruminations lifted her foot from the accelerator as surely as they had lifted her eyes from the road. The driver behind her flashed his headlamps again and again, frustrated in his desperation to overtake by a series of suicide bends. Normally he would pass everything, anywhere, but not on these tight bends at night. 'Bloody tourists,' he thought. 'Why don't you pull over if you want to watch the view!' and cursed out loud as he flashed his lights and hooted his horn.

Startled from her reveries, Newman accelerated sharply, pulling her car up to a speed acceptable to local travellers. Rounding a further series of bends, moving faster and faster, Newman's pulse beat quickly in her chest as she determined to make amends to the trail of inconvenienced, irritated drivers.

Out of the dark bushes to her right, a shape moved fast and precise into the beam of her headlamps. Braking as she jumped, the form of a running deer filled her view as she heard and felt the thump of the collision. The car skidded to a halt. Newman sat and gripped the steering wheel, staring straight ahead, unable and unwilling to move, blood thumping in her skull. She knew she had hit the deer. The metal of the car felt and sounded somehow soft, muffled as it hit flesh and bone. The impact was velvet but vicious and she knew she would for ever own the pain

Robert's grandparents, 1905. Robert's father, William, is wearing a kilt

Robert with
Mother, Father
and Tina. Robert,
sitting on his
mother's knee, is
one year old

Robert at fifteen (*front row, centre*) was captain of the swimming team
at King Edward's School, Birmingham (1945)

Robert's twenty-first birthday party. Birthday boy, replete with new
moustache, sits in the centre of the front row (1951)

Robert's parents, Eva and William Pine (*c*.late 1950s). Eva wears the ceremonial chain and cloak as Mayor of Oldbury. William wears the spouse's insignia or, as his children used to tease, 'the Mayoress's chain'

A night out. Still favouring the moustache, Robert sits in the centre of the group. He is accompanied by his parents, Tina and Frank, his older and more affluent travelling companion on frequent trips to Scotland (*c*.1952)

Robert Pine receives his first stripe. He is now a lance corporal, though his father cannot quite believe it (*c.*1950)

Robert and his girlfriend win a prize for buying the 1,000th ticket at the local cinema (*c.*1952)

The first class Robert taught (1954)

Robert moves to teach at a junior secondary school (1956)

Robert in 1956

Robert's wedding to his first wife, Doreen, on 13 October 1956

On holiday in Scotland with his children, Fiona and Duncan (*c.*1972)

LEFT: Ready for the party.
Hogmanay Carnival Dance,
Otley (1981)

BELOW: Second-hand Rose.
Robert and Jean in fancy dress,
Harrogate (1982)

inflicted and damage caused. Agony and carnage was what Newman intuitively expected to find and she could not move, would not move to witness the death throes of the animal which must surely be writhing on the cold road under the glare of her car lights.

The convoy of cars behind Newman had also come to an abrupt halt. Several drivers abandoned their cars and ran to the grass verge where the deer had been heading. Some, more adventurous than others, leapt the fence and waded through the undergrowth. Eventually, the posse gave up on the deer chase and returned to Newman's car where they stood around and poked at the near side head lamp and wing. The self-nominated spokesman, the same man who had been careering towards road rage only minutes earlier, rattled Newman's car window with his knuckles, startling her from her frozen state. The man told Newman that the car wing was badly bashed and the head lamp smashed. He asked her where she was going then advised that she should be all right to complete her journey but she should follow him, just to be safe. He was going through Tarbert so she could tail him all the way. The help was given in a manner that would brook no alternative. She had to follow him and that was that. He stepped back from her car and then returned to make his final comment with a leery smile, 'By the way, you almost got the stag. Next time, don't brake and steer to the left.'

As the anonymous male helper pulled his car out, Newman noticed it was a dilapidated, ancient heap and one headlamp was not working. She followed the mobile pile of junk, nerves jumping, pulling anxiously at the gears and steering wheel. Her body and head felt light, the signs of mild shock, and she made a mental note to have a cup of sweet tea and something to eat before the anticipated brandy.

As Newman and her rescuer swept down the hill at Stonefield Castle and past the half-obscured walls of Ashens Cottage, she thought again of Robert and Jean. The incident with the deer had left her emotional and repentant. No matter what else was in her mind she kept receiving images of the stag dragging his broken rear through the whins, bleeding as he moved, hirpling slower and slower to an inevitable lonely death. She admonished herself for staying away from the Pines, for treating them as a peep show where trouble would emerge. She had been watching and waiting for the Pines, as outsiders, to be ostracised and rejected. She expected Bob's arty ideas to get him into difficulty with the down-to-earth fisher folk and the cautious shopkeepers. Newman knew she could have been a friend to the Pines instead of their personal, unannounced *sans culottes*. They had all been around Tarbert for five years; it would be embarrassing to talk of the past now. Bob and Jean would wonder why she had waited for so long to talk with them and would ask questions. The Pines had done so well in settling here and now they were going to move to the edge of the village. Newman thought of the stag calling out in pain and suffered the low ache of dread. Newman had a premonition of trouble.

11 To the Land of Loss and Gain

And when at last my days are passed on this shore of life's sea
I wonder will my children wish they had talked to me.
REBECCA PINE IN 'DEAR FATHER . . .'

Leeds, England. 1978.
Jean Todd had just moved to the Leeds area. She joined the Caledonian Society to make friends and because she enjoyed the spirit and style of the dancing. The Scottish and Caledonian Societies throughout the north of England met up frequently to host events, share resources and generally join together people with common interests. In addition, there were Burns Federations, Celtic and Rangers FC Supporters Clubs, Scottish regiments' reunions, friends of the Edinburgh Festival, Scottish clubs, pubs, football teams and rugby teams. A large and complex network of Caledonians had developed in the most unlikely setting of towns like Harrogate and Hull, Huddersfield and York, Leeds and Bradford. Robert had also taken to Scottish country dancing, having joined a local Caledonian Society. His timing, balance and sense of order served him well as he displayed an aptitude for, as well as pleasure in, this activity. The Society also led him to meet many Scottish people. Some had been in England for twenty or thirty years but retained the heart of their accents and their obvious love of the place they considered to be home. Robert stood out as someone with no direct birth link to Scotia but who was as enthusiastic as the next Society member and a better dancer than most. Jean and Robert's interests in dancing, music and poetry had drawn them into the same wider circle.

Mrs Jean Todd had lived in the east of Scotland, first

Edinburgh then Port Seaton, with her husband and their three children – Jackie, Kirsty and Campbell. She was highly educated and well read with interests in poetry, music, drama and, of course, dancing. Jean was an attractive and vivacious woman with an energy towards the creative. Polite in her manner and bearing, she had a ready sense of humour exposed by a wicked smile. The presence of these ingredients in the being of a disciplined school teacher (which she was) produced an attractive, vivacious chemistry for many people.

Jean had fled south to England with her children. To her great hurt and loss, her husband had succumbed to the draw of booze, drinking more and more till addiction took hold. Jean's marriage had started well but slowly and surely drifted down and into the malaise, sadness and violence of an alcoholic stupor. Jean fought hard and sore to keep her marriage going through years of unreliability, disappointment and increasing desperation. When shortage of funds, aggression and chronic unhappiness began to affect her children, Jean decided it was time to leave. Gathering her three children together with case-loads of clothes and little else, she headed southwards, not sure where she was going, with no job awaiting her and no home. Such a move would provide Jean with the opportunity to give her children a better life and once she had decided this, she simply did not hesitate.

By the time Robert met her, Jean and the children were secure in accommodation and she had found work in a nursery. The difficulties she had faced such a short time before were not evident to Robert, who met an attractive and articulate woman. When the Caledonia Societies held joint events, members would tend to take along their partners, even those who were not normally interested in Dashing White Sergeants, Gay Gordons or reels of any description. These were socials, a night out, and people came along to relax and enjoy themselves. Doreen Pine was not at all interested in Scottish country dancing, or anything Scottish as far as Robert knew. Doreen had her job, her children, her sisters, her badminton and left Robert to get on with the rest. Jean Todd had no partner either. On nights when their two Societies came together, Robert and Jean were among the few single people and while spreading their company around the dance floor, often ended up dancing with each other. They danced well together, found an increasing list of common interests and looked forward to meeting up again. In short, Robert and Jean had become friends, just good friends.

~

Bradford, England. 1979.
The night was as wet as it could be in the north of England. The gutters were running with water which collected here and there where the drains were blocked. The reservoirs spreading out from the pavement lifted and floated the debris of the day, the litter which marked the lifestyle of the people.

Golden Wonder, Coca Cola, Benson and Hedges were advertised as were the sexual habits of the neighbourhood. A child's nappy, folded and full, lay like an immovable rock around which floated the occasional prophylactic, bending and moving in the current of the rain like a lonely water snake. These residential streets of Bradford had become the stomping ground of what passed as a sex industry in those parts. After the hour of darkness, women would appear on corners and under the weak, amber fuzz that was street lighting and wait for the men in their cars. An ancient trade built on poverty and lust, fed by the inability of people to relate to people. Prostitution in Bradford was a murky, degrading business and no effort was made to claim otherwise. During the light hours the same streets opened the doors of their houses and revealed families, children and the day-to-day exigencies of life – school, work in the factories, the tick man, white bread and tea from the corner shop, children playing, parents rowing, visits to the pub and nights in front of the TV, eating fried food from plates balanced on knees. Then darkness would fall, bringing out the prostitutes and drawing the mean-spirited, foul cloud of cruising desperadoes, voyeurs, the impotent, aggressors and worse. Prostitution was cheap in Bradford, as was life. From time to time a woman would be raped and murdered in some vacant lot, discarded along with the other soiled and spent goods. Local residents would raise an outcry and appeal to the authorities to clear the area and give them back their neighbourhood. The families asked for security and safety, claiming that as their right and as a normal life. Some suspected that their normal life had already arrived and did nothing.

On the periphery of this area were several halls, meeting places, safe pubs and other venues. That rainy night, the local

Highland society were having an evening of poetry and songs to be rounded off with a dance. Robert was in attendance as part of a group invited from Harrogate. Many months earlier he had damaged his knee with lasting effect. This meant he was ruled out of playing badminton for an entire year. By that time, Robert was club captain and played several times each week, including league competitions. The captaincy was handed on to a young Turk, part of a group of rising stars who demonstrated considerable skill as well as peak fitness. Robert enjoyed badminton, not just for the sport which he adored, but also for the social aspect, the organisation and the team work. He feared he would never regain his position from the younger crew. His inability to play took a large chunk out of his life and he replaced it with increased involvement in other interests.

Drama, poetry and literature still played a major part in defining Robert Pine. While he would never lose his love of the arts, he needed an activity less sedentary and found that his dodgy knee could cope with the demands of Scottish country dancing. This discovery was not made on medical advice but by trial and error. Those who knew Bob Pine superficially or as a passing acquaintance often did not spot the quixotic part of his character. In truth, he had little regard for caution when it applied to his own safety. Robert believed life was for living and that meant some personal risks at times. So he was to be found on several nights each week skipping, jumping, turning, twisting, stamping and twirling, all on a knee too weak to tolerate the rigours of badminton. The doctor had ruled out the racquet sport but had omitted to apply any such ban to the dances of Scotland. Maybe the doctor had been told of the hobby and imagined gentle, sedate waltzes rather than the warlike ferocity of the reels or the marathon proportions of Strip the Willow. Then again, the doctor may have given more comprehensive advice had Robert bothered to mention the dancing.

As so often in Robert Pine's life, a problem and a denial had metamorphosed into a discovery and a gift. What had started as a poor substitute for badminton, a kind of ersatz sport, had transformed into a lifelong love, bad knee and all. He had already made many friends through the Scottish country dancing. In some respects he was a rare commodity – a healthy, handsome, fit and knowledgeable male dancer who wanted to dance rather than being dragged reluctantly along by a determined wife. Robert was popular, particularly among the women.

Doreen Pine did not dance, leastwise not as a hobby. As Robert's knee had cracked, so a gap had appeared in his marriage. The couple had been taken unawares, suddenly realising that beyond the domestic their only shared activity had been badminton. Overnight, Robert and Doreen lost their shared social life. The couple seemed to go their separate ways constantly to meet again at bedtime or over the crowded breakfast table. Robert had not anticipated this development that day in the doctor's surgery as the long-term prognosis on his knee was declared. He had been too busy mourning the loss of part of his life to see the hole about to be blasted through his marriage. As with the most acute problems in relationships, the realisation grew after the problem, after they had changed. After nearly a quarter of a century, Robert Pine had learned a sad truth about his marriage and was beginning to feel lonely. Doreen seemed to be getting on with it, as far as Robert knew. It did not occur to him to discuss the problems with her and he did not expect a sympathetic hearing. Robert thought of Doreen as strong-willed, disciplined and with a clear view of what she expected from life. With the children, her job, her home and her sisters, Robert expected Doreen to be quite satisfied. For years she had not grumbled as he spent night after night pursuing his arts. Would she notice the difference now? Robert did not think so.

The night in Bradford was jolly but unremarkable. Robert was having a good time and had met up with a number of friends he had not seen for a long while. Tea had been served and the activities ceased for an intermission. Robert walked among the fellow members, cup and saucer in hand, stopping now and then to chat. He was standing at a table where a group of women were seated. They were teasing him about making sure their names were on his dance card for later and he replied in kind, while making a mental note to make sure and dance with all of the group. Robert felt a cold, damp draught beside him as if someone had opened a trap door by his feet, letting in a blast of Bradford's rain-soaked wind. Looking round, he found Jean Todd standing at his side. He was pleased, though surprised, since Jean's group had not been invited that evening. She had just arrived, late in the proceedings. Smiling at Robert she said, 'I thought I'd find you here. Can I have a word with you, please?'

Fetching Jean a cup of tea to combat the night's chill, Robert was a little troubled, though intrigued, by the purpose of Jean's lengthy journey and the subject of the proposed chat. Put simply, he did not know what to expect.

Jean invited Robert to accompany her on a trip to Germany. The Caledonia Society she was a member of was to travel to various communities on an exchange visit, centring on folk dancing. Would Robert accompany her as her dancing partner? As friends?

Before the tea was finished, Robert and Jean had planned to go on the holiday together, departing one week later.

~

Leeds, England. 1979.

Robert's separation from Doreen was acrimonious. On his side, he could see the nuances and shades of every picture. He believed that Doreen could only see right or wrong and little in-between. In this instance, Robert had to accept he was the one taking the action which called for judgement and did not blame Doreen for treating him with a measure of cold disdain. She felt that their life together was no more or less than should be expected. Robert found it hard to believe that Doreen was incapable of imagining a better relationship or an enhanced quality of life but had to conclude that that was how it appeared to her. Words and phrases such as tunnel vision, stoic, a brick, would occur to him as he tried to understand his estranged wife from a distance. These attributes had seen them through hard and difficult times and kept him on the straight and narrow when tempted to fly off into the slipstream of some flight of fancy. He admired, still, those qualities in Doreen but, now, those same defining characteristics set limits on his partner of the last quarter of a century, causing her to reject him unilaterally and brook no caveat, even where their children were concerned.

Robert suspected Doreen would be incapable of thinking of him or hear mention of his name without sending out a signal of total disapproval and dismissal. Whether deliberate or subconscious, the signal would be clear and effective especially with their children, Fiona and Duncan. Robert feared for his relationship with his children. They were so close to their mother and would move closer still now that he had moved out of the home. The elder, Fiona, was particularly close to her mother and would feel the hurt and anger Doreen was experiencing. Fiona was a young adult now and bright, very bright. Able enough to comprehend the way of the world and the sadness of adults with adults, no matter how hard they tried. The young woman was also assertive and single-minded, having inherited a major slice of her personality from Doreen. Duncan was still young and less insistent than his older sibling. He had developed the tendency to follow her lead, an approach which had served him well through his vulnerable childhood years. Would the son follow the sister still in this matter of their father? Robert feared he would and knew exactly whose side his daughter would take.

~

Harrogate, England. 1980.
Jean and the children loved Harrogate. It was a big and small town rolled into one. It could support all the needs of life, particularly of growing children, while being intimate enough for them to feel that they belonged. The children could see that their mother was happy and Bob Pine was kind and gentle. They had come to know Bob Pine well for quite some time before he and their mother decided to live together. They liked this mother, happy and relaxed, and loved the way that she and Bob did things together. Their mother had always been there for them, especially during the bad times in Scotland but now there seemed to be more of her somehow.

The world will assume that Robert and Jean consummated their relationship in Germany. After all, there was more than a hint of romance in the spontaneity of Jean's invitation – searching Robert out and she, the woman, inviting him, the man, to go on holiday. The Women's Liberation Movement, the pill, sexual politics and more had gone a good way to moving the power dynamics between men and women, but not that far. Jean was ahead of her time in being so forthright. She was also being honest and the two went on holiday as friends and returned as friends, albeit a good deal closer. So, the world would be wrong in assuming a torrid fortnight in Germany with passion being interrupted by the necessity of eating and dancing, the latter being the actual purpose of the trip. Jean and Robert discovered that they had a great deal in common, sharing all the same interests in the arts and having an endless stream of conversation.

On their return to England the friendship continued and prospered. Robert felt his marriage to Doreen slipping further and further away, reducing to the domestic mundane at worst and shared interest in the children at best. Life with Doreen was a combination of shared necessities – home, income, childcare. His friendship with Jean was a chemistry of shared dreams – art, literature, dance, music, poetry, travel. Jean and Robert became friends first and foremost and then became lovers.

~

Harrogate, England. 1981.

Jean loved her life and with her recently formed family was living it to the full. She had a job in a local hospital, running a crèche. The type of work was not as demanding as the teaching she was trained for but she could not work in formal education in England. She had been trained in Scotland and would require to have her qualification accredited as she would if she had moved to Australia, France or other distinct nations. Besides, she found the work with younger children an inspiration and the difference in salary was not that important now. Money had never been that important to Jean: people and life were her priorities. People, starting with her children.

One day she was returning home in the middle of the afternoon as expected. Entering her house her mind was on the children's return from school, what they would eat, homework and play time with their mother. Robert was at work and would not be back till later in the evening, so the four of them would have time together. Entering the house, something struck her as unusual but exactly *what*, she could not specify. By nature a trusting person, Jean found herself walking through the house, room to room, trying to get a sense of what was different. Everything looked the same till she spotted some blood in the bathroom. Perplexed and a little alarmed, she wandered to other rooms, frowning and still not having a clue. She almost tripped over a chair which was not in its normal place and was lying on its side. Bending over to pick it up, she noticed smudges of blood on the woodwork.

Something made Jean look up. What she saw would prove to be a crucial part of the matrix when later, much later, she began to understand what had happened in her home that day when the family were out. The trap to the attic was open. Jean was not superstitious nor was she an addict of the film industry which held dark lofts as one key location for sinister events and spooks. Jean did not imagine tense, melodramatic music growing in volume, heralding the arrival of the evil one. She did not even suspect a break-in or burglary. Jean was puzzled as to why anyone, even the family, would want to climb up and into that dusty enclave. She knew that all that was up there was some empty suitcases, piping left from some plumbing work long before their arrival and a few battered cardboard boxes. Robert had brought the boxes, explaining that they contained old clothes which he really should give to Oxfam. Had Robert decided on that drive to the charity shop? Surely not, he was meant to be in York all day.

Later that night Robert returned much as expected except that on his eyebrow he wore freshly inserted stitches. When Jean asked him about the incident his reply was uncharacteristically vague. She did not press for further information, assuming that her man was embarrassed by his fall.

～

Harrogate, England. 1981
The Girl Guides is one of those organisations which many people believe in but few contribute towards. There is something comforting, even for the most agnostic individual, to know that young girls are motivated to wear the uniform, behave by the rules and learn all the Guides have to teach before moving on to more complex adult pursuits. The Guides are somehow clear of the lavatorial humour which follows the Boy Scouts and the regrettable revelations, usually in the Sunday tabloids, supporting the contention that jokes about Scout masters are actually true, at least now and then. Not so the Guides, making it hard to criticise this phase of female childhood when there is a motivation to obey rules and work to a regime. So many people believe the Girl Guides to be an organisation, at worst harmless and at best useful, though few assist in making them happen.

Jean became a Guide Leader and was pleased to give of her time to foster a wider range of interests and skills in young women, helping them to develop an understanding of life and an appreciation of beauty in all its forms. Being a Guide Leader took up a great deal of Jean's time on regular nights each week. Robert supported Jean in this activity as she, in turn, supported him in the pursuit of singular interests. On Guide nights, Robert would make a point of staying at home and looking after Jackie, Kirsty and Campbell. By the time Jean returned to the house on these nights, the children would be fed, washed, read to and bedded down. Arriving home, weary but full of chat, she often blessed her good fortune at finding a man who was interested in her interests and on whom she could rely for help. The two adults would share a late-night cup of tea, listening to classical music on the radio, a restful end to a satisfying day.

The night the heating system broke down, there was nothing for it but to end the Girl Guides' session early, the hall being too draughty and cold. Frustrated by the technical hitch, Jean was secretly pleased to be getting home to her partner earlier than planned. She entered the house with a smile, expecting to catch Kirsty still out of bed or Robert washing up the supper dishes. The house was silent and the children were tucked up in bed and, if not sleeping, were quiet enough to suggest contentment. Walking up the stairs Jean went directly to her bedroom from which noises emanated, indicating Robert's presence. Going through the door, she caught sight of Robert, dressed only in his underwear, hurriedly rolling up some clothing which she recognised to be from her side of the wardrobe.

Jean's inquisitive frown posed the question with no need for words. Robert responded right away, explaining it was just a joke. Quickly he added that he was trying out some outfits for a fancy dress party coming up soon – just whiling away the time until she came home. Robert kept speaking all the way to the kitchen, the kettle, over two pots of tea and later in bed. Jean was not sure about the whole affair but she trusted her partner and, besides, she never had the opportunity to ask questions.

~

North Wales. 1981.
The golf course was beautiful, offering the type of space and settled, wild terrain only a rural area could sustain. Robert thought the best courses were in Scotland though the more isolated parts of England and Wales produced some gems. He had already organised trips to Dalmahoy, Gullane and the East Lothian courses, Southerness and the Dumfries courses and

now it was the turn of North Wales. Everyone agreed the Scottish courses were best but now it was time to turn attention to locations closer to home. So Robert found himself on this glorious course in North Wales playing his usual competent game. He had been appointed Rabbits' Captain as a mark of his tendency to sparkle as often as his game collapsed. As with most interests, he had proven to be an enthusiast and ever-ready to turn up on weekends.

Golf allows time for reflection and that day in Wales, Robert was feeling excited and invigorated as he contemplated a weekend of golf, bridge and the company of very good friends. Perhaps it happened because his mind was on a place far away or maybe it was just the damp, greasy grass. Either way, he twisted and damaged his leg, falling over and calling out in pain. His playing partner recognised that Robert was under some duress and agony and hurried off in search of assistance. Golf being a sport attracting a certain type of player, a doctor happened to be on the course and was soon ferried to the injured man's side. The diagnosis was swift and precise – Robert had broken his leg and needed hospital treatment immediately.

The doctor departed, having a round of golf to complete, leaving Robert in the care of his companion. Now standing, Robert tentatively tested his weight on the broken leg and confirmed that it was seriously damaged. Wincing, he looked in the direction of the club house and his car. He would have to walk a long distance, cutting across several fairways and negotiating thick, rough, sand bunkers and two streams. He then looked in the direction of the next green and the official route round the course. With a shrug, he pulled a golf club out of his bag, lined up to the small, white ball and struck it crisply towards the pin.

Ignoring the protestations of his playing companion, Robert completed his round of golf and scored almost as well as he could have hoped with two sound legs. Changing out of his spiked shoes, he drove five miles to the nearest hospital where he had his leg set in plaster from ankle to thigh. As the casualty doctor sympathised with his bad luck and the severity of the break, Robert asked him if he had ever been to Scotland.

~

Harrogate, England. 1981.

Hambro Life Insurance Company was an understanding employer. The senior managers may have adopted a different
attitude had Robert been a poor salesman or intended to remain
on their payroll for years to come. Trouble was that the plaster
on his broken leg prevented Robert from putting on trousers
and he was left with the puzzle of how to attend work and go
about in public without being charged with indecency. This
difficulty may have proved insurmountable for most people but
Robert had an immediate and effective solution right there in
his own wardrobe. He wore a kilt.

People enjoy the unusual and unexpected. Highland dress was
a solution which enhanced, rather than impeded, his sales over
that period in Harrogate and he carried the part well,
resplendent in beard, plastered leg and kilt. The plaster was
removed some months later but the beard and the kilt remained.

~

Leeds, England. 1982.

The photographer had accessed a vantage point in a building
overlooking the vast plaza which marked the centre of the
polytechnic's campus. From this viewpoint he had been able to
record much of the day's activities unimpeded by parking
double-decker buses or straying, unthinking onlookers. More
often than not, he had to use his zoom lens to focus in on the
performers. Even the group events could be easily covered from
this height and the resultant photographs would look as if he
had been on the same level as the dancers when he opened and
closed the shutter. The photographer had a programme of the
day's order of events but from this elevation he could not hear
any announcements. He had ticked the various turns off his list
in the hope that he was keeping up to speed and his list
describing the subject of the photographs was accurate. He was
awaiting the next performance which seemed to be taking an
inordinate time to set up.

The park was awash with vivid colours in a manner contra-
dicting the dank, industrial image of Leeds. The Twenty-ninth
Festival of Scottish Country Dancing was taking place outdoors
and in a city renowned for its one-way systems, urban routes
and concrete. Hundreds of people had descended onto the
grassy, level surface and appeared to be dashing around with no

purpose. Stewards hurried among the throng, speaking to group leaders and marking out allocated space. Some of the women wore light-coloured ball gowns, cut to knee or mid-calf length and marked by a sash of tartan across their chests. The wide skirts of the dresses flared out, showing the edge of petticoats. Others preferred long tartan skirts with blouses, plain in their pure white while demonstrating extravagance by the detail of their stitching. There were Highland dancers in kilts, plaids and pumps, hopping and turning to the skirl of bagpipes. The warlike wailing tunes for flings and sword dances could be heard by the photographer up on his perch. Men in kilts and baggy white shirts milled around, hands gripping the top of their sporrans, unaccustomed to their pocketless outfits.

As the dancers waited for their signal to start, Robert caught Jean's eye and smiled. They were in different dance sets but very much together. Robert grinned and winked. Jean returned the compliment with a nod and a smile. At that, the platform-risen accordions let loose the pre-emptive chord, calling the participants to attention, holding hands and poised. The next chord brought synchronised male bows and female curtsies, flowing in a wave across the square.

High up on the building opposite, the photographer had worked out his next task. The scale of this demonstration was so vast he would require to use a wide-angled lens and take several snaps to ensure coverage of the vista. He had a plan to join the photographs so that the whole scene would be visible in one elongated, panoramic view. The craftsman would produce a very fine picture and he was hopeful of attracting some sales. A postcard, maybe, or framed enlargements. Only those involved or fanatics for this folk art would be interested in the latter. The potential market would not be large but the mark-up was certain to be several hundred per cent. Each photograph would be laid on a dark green, velveteen card and mounted in plain black, silver or gold gilt frames with the price increasing correspondingly. Every kiltie would ponder the options and aspire to own the more expensive gold-coloured frame, knowing certain other Society members who would splash out the coin for the privilege. 'Keeping up with the MacTavishes, hee, hee, hee,' the photographer cackled to his own amusement.

Calculating the cost to the public, allowing for discounts and special discounts (the latter being less than the former), the professional voyeur lined up his next shot, aiming the centre-lens marker directly on a tall, slim fellow at the core of the dancers.

Standing back from the mounted camera, the photographer looked down on the rows and columns of tartan-clad hordes, poised and immobile, stretching from the main college building to the pavements and farther. From his eyrie he could see everything but hear nothing save the whistle of the wind and the occasional warbling of a pigeon resting on a nearby window ledge. From the left wing, up, then down, each consecutive line, he began to count the dancers, calculating his maximum possible income. Two pigeons jostled for space in the corner of an otherwise vacant sill and the weaker of the two fluttered its wings before hopping out into space and flying off to find rest elsewhere.

The still life of Caledonian devotees moved as one, first with a bow or curtsy, before taking off in all directions – round and around, up and down, in and out. Like mad, kilted dervishes, throwing their arms out and kicking their heels – round and around, up and down, in and out – silently working a rhythm known to them all but to no one else. Caught in his fascination with the madness of it all, the photographer forgot about his camera and gaped, chin hanging loose. Regaining his composure and recalling his purpose, he quickly bent to the camera which he kick-started to click and whirr rapidly.

'God Almighty,' he grumbled, 'there are so many of them about. Much more than you'd think.'

～

Tarbert, Argyll. 1982.
Robert and Jean had discovered so much in common they soon became hungry to spend more time on living and less on working to live. Sandwiched between their good-tempered debates on east or west coast of Scotland, they made some intricate financial calculations. They concluded that they could afford to set themselves up in a home and small business but would need to keep earning for some years, particularly till the children had left school and established themselves. They both agreed that the level and style of work should not be allowed to intrude on the quality of their lives, otherwise why bother moving at all?

They intended to pursue some venture which supported Robert's art and they knew this would be high risk on the economic front although low risk on the personal front. Ideally, they were searching for a large-scale operation allowing them to use their skills and expertise as well as being engrossed within the cultural activities they craved. So the visit to Oban had potential as a social and Scottish country dance centre wherein they could exploit their qualifications as dance teachers and use their contacts throughout the network of Caledonia Societies in England, America, Canada and further afield. Busloads of devotees would arrive from the South, delighted to ceilidh late into the night and recuperate by day, touring the jagged coves of Argyll and the soft, rumbling hills of Lorn. The business plan was sound but the price was too high and Robert had felt uneasy around the Oban area.

That first visit to Tarbert, coming down from the Crow's Nest and meeting Jean and the children was one of the happiest moments of Robert's life. The family's unanimous agreement to move to the village was perfect. Again, from the disappointment of Oban, built on such high hopes, Robert Pine had discovered prospects in Tarbert, where he had expected to find none. 'A lucky man,' he thought. 'I'm such a lucky man.'

They would buy the shop, like many old seaside buildings small in scale but enough for their plans. To meet the overheads, they would sell a range of basic goods – sugar, milk, bread, biscuits, sweets and Sunday newspapers – while gradually introducing books, art and poetry, increasing those lines while their reputation grew. They expected that the shop alone would not bring enough income so they would buy a house wherein they could provide a bed and breakfast. This latter enterprise would keep them ticking over through the summer months but was not to be their long-term mainstay. Robert and Jean had much grander plans.

It was November 1982 and it had not been a good year – the Falklands conflict, three million unemployed in Britain, bombs in Hyde Park, massacres in Palestine, Rainer Fassbinder dead at thirty-six years of age. Robert, Jean and the children returned from their visit to Tarbert to their home in Harrogate pregnant with plans for a new future.

~

Tarbert, Argyll. 1983.

Springside Cottage was on the Pier Road, wedged into the hillside under the shadow of Tarbert Castle to the rear. To the fore it looked out on East Loch – that bending, twisting part of Loch Fyne, which carves out the harbour and beauty of the village. Across from the front garden, the rocky inlet of The Dooklinne nestled under the wooded slopes of Barfad, sheltering the castle and estate of Stonefield from the highest-placed house of Tarbert. At night, the light on MacArthur's Island, a small mole of land, would shine green and steady, less dramatic than the flashing red, marking sharp rocks nearby.

Jean and Robert had fallen in love with the cottage as they had with the village. They were used to a certain level of comfort and convenience in their home and started on refurbishing the cottage and the shop with a vengeance. Their unbridled enthusiasm gave them added vigour, enough to live the life they had planned while converting the house. They expected the decades of paint on woodwork, the lack of a shower and the absence of central heating. In the shop they drew breath as they removed layer upon layer of linoleum from the sinking floors but were amused enough to stop and count – seven layers in all – and imagined how many years of replenishing the floor-covering that number represented. It was hard but honest work.

The family appreciated the quaint style of these older West Highland cottages. They had come from a part of the country where the major building companies were erecting vast swathes of coloured breeze-block shoe boxes. They much preferred the idiosyncrasies of Springside – even when they discovered that the stairwell was unusually broad on the first floor but gradually narrowed with the descent till an adult had to turn sideways to proceed. An average-size tea tray could not be carried upstairs without being turned on its edge. Add the severe turn and the stairs were downright dangerous. They would have to go.

A local joiner was engaged to rebuild the stairs. As with many a willing tradesman he was neither qualified nor trained. He turned his hand to joinery, was relatively cheap in an expensive market and was available. Most days Robert and the joiner would work together and they had reached the stage of building the new staircase. One day, Robert and Jean visited Glasgow, planning to return in the evening. On the way back, Robert fretted about how much work would have been done, the joiner having been left to his own devices. Back at Springside, the couple were delighted to note that the stairs had been joined and a note was left warning them against use while the glue was setting. Robert felt a little guilty at his suspicious thoughts. Sharing a recuperative pot of tea with Jean, something troubled Robert and he could not relax. Returning to the stairwell he looked with a focused, less expectant eye and the puzzle was revealed – the stairs had been put together upside down. He worked late into the night dismantling the steps before the glue hardened for ever.

Robert no longer felt guilty. He had learned an important lesson on one price he would pay for his idyll in Argyll.

~

Tarbert, Argyll. 1983.
The June sky was painted the lightest of blues and held fluffed pillows of white clouds moving rapidly in from the loch. Robert sat in his car at the end of the Battery, a thick pad on his lap, sketching Springside Cottage in the distance with the castle looming high overhead. He would have preferred a perch outside but the vantage point was exposed and always subject to disruptive fluttering winds. So he sat in his car and drew his home.

That morning he had wandered over the rocks, beyond the view of the village, needing time on his own. It was not necessary to go far to be alone in this part of the world. Scrambling over the scrub and the crags he had reached Shell Beach in a matter of minutes. The mass of pink, silver and shiny grey of shells underfoot glittered in the sun and crackled as he walked. It was easy to feel destructive walking on such fragile morsels, though generations had stood here looking out to sea and the shells kept replenishing themselves. Robert had not heard an explanation of how the shells came to be there in the first instance. There were so many at that one point and so few elsewhere along the shore, it looked as if someone had harvested the flesh and discarded the casings. He preferred the notion of a chosen resting place, a shells' graveyard where they came to die and lie with their genus. Graveyards were much on his mind that day.

Mother had died a few weeks earlier, on 27 May. Eva Pine

had been frail for some time and had been lovingly looked after by sister Tina. Mother had outlived Father, her William, by fourteen years. Robert had mourned for Father, his spiritual guide and mentor. For many months he had been fixated by memories, little coloured scenarios from the man's life. As with all bereavements, Robert had felt sorry for himself in his loss but always returned to images of Father with Mother, his Eva. How his Father adored the woman and how he had taken pride in her success. The day she became Mayor of Oldbury. The official engagements when Father would accompany her in all her regalia and he with his own, smaller chain – the Mayoress's chain, Tina and Robert would tease. Thinking then of Mother becoming a Member of the British Empire, Robert felt that part of that MBE belonged to Father. William had supported his wife, written speeches, given advice, held her hand and encouraged her at every turn. He did so, not through obligation, but through devotion.

Only in the years since Father's death had Robert truly realised his parents were a couple, who lived for each other and because of each other. These thoughts were returned to him afresh as he mourned his Mother. Robert smiled into the glare of sun on the sea and thought, 'Behind every strong woman there is a clever, loving man.'

With both parents dead, Robert knew a part of him was gone for ever. He remembered a night as a child, summoned out of bed and standing there on the cold, hard floor. A question he did not understand and an answer given through fear. He would answer that question differently now but the chance was gone for ever. Robert stood on Shell Beach and cried in grief for parents he loved who would never know him, their only son.

~

Scotch Corner, Durham, England. 1983.
'I really must find out the history of this place and why it's called Scotch Corner. Probably because so many Scots met up here on their way South to murder, pillage or rape. Should find out the details, though.' Robert was repeating a motivational reminder to himself as he steered between the lorries parked around the café, heading for the road to the South.

This was a road he had travelled many times, though not often with Jean. They chatted about the prospects of this being their last time going south to England together, evaluating the few reasons they may have for future journeys. The chances were they would drive down the other, west coast, heading to Oldbury to visit Tina or some friends. They were severing the ties with Harrogate through this visit; tidying up some business before settling to their life in Argyll.

Robert had been a single man again for a couple of months, his divorce from Doreen being finalised on 16 September 1983. Divorce had felt like a non-event, being expected, and yet it was strangely liberating in spite of being expected. The symbolism of the finality of divorce had an ominous solemnity about it and surprised no one more than Robert Pine himself. Fiona and Duncan had moved nearer to Leeds to be closer to their centres of work and play. Robert imagined his daughter travelling often to visit her mother, without giving any thought to Argyll and her father. The stop at the motorway café had only served to remind Robert of distant, happier times with his young family. He loved Fiona and Duncan and ached for their company and their smiles. He wanted to know what was happening in their lives and for them to feel they could trust him, taking their problems to their father for help. Robert did not blame Fiona and Duncan but wished they needed to know what was happening in their father's life.

Robert felt more satisfied, challenged, supported and inspired with Jean than he had for years, however. Jean shared his interests and his dreams. Robert shared her interests and her dreams. They were a matching pair. His life was going well yet he mourned why, as happens so often, there needed to be a personal cost paid in full. The balancing act of human existence: winter and summer; agony and ecstasy; love and hate; life and death.

Robert knew he wanted to spend his life with Jean. Not given to thinking too seriously about the far-away future, he could acknowledge to himself that even if the fires burned out and they passed into a cold old age together, Jean would be the one he would choose as a companion. Just as he had chosen her as friend, lover, partner and muse.

Tarbert was working out well for Robert, Jean and the children. Their lives were full of discovery, joy and plans. The villagers had been a little withdrawn to start with but no more than villagers anywhere. In fact, the Pine family had already made friends. Tarbert was in the West Highlands, however, and some of the people were known to be rather conservative, not to say strait-laced, in Robert and Jean's opinion. The couple had been cautious to consider local values, traditions and expectations and Jean and the children had all legally changed their names to Pine before arriving at the village. They saw no deception in this device since they were a family in every sense. Robert and Jean shared the worry that some of the villagers might think badly of them, and the children, had they discovered that they were unmarried, living together, 'in sin'. While the description amused Robert and brought a twinkle to Jean's eye, they wanted to be accepted by everyone in Tarbert and not judged because of something as inconsequential as the lack of a marriage certificate. There was no reason for that now.

To protect the sensibilities of the Tarbert folk, to save them from moral outrage and shock, Robert and Jean decided to get legally wed. They were married in truth and simplicity in Harrogate, England on 30 November 1983 – St Andrew's Day, of course.

12 Susan Goes the Whole Hog

For 'tis the eternal law
That first in beauty should be the first in might.
JOHN KEATS IN 'HYPERION. A FRAGMENT. I'

A83 road near Inveraray, Scotland. 1988.
The road was almost deserted and this freedom was one of the few good reasons Robert could imagine for getting up so early in the morning. As Robert drove, Jean chatted, animated and excited. As well as being a morning person to her husband's night-owl disposition, Jean was looking forward to the day ahead. The road to Inveraray was so familiar to Robert that he sometimes forgot which landmark he had passed or what hamlet came next. He had driven this road often enough and remained alert, always expecting the unexpected and refusing the seduction of the view.

In his previous life, before Tarbert, he had driven many thousands of miles each year as a salesman and branch manager. The hills and dales of Yorkshire were as common territory to him as the often manic and always boring motorways, scattered on the map like some crazed arterial formation linking the main organs of the country. The back roads of rural England had been difficult to drive and colleagues would often grumble that they could do more work and sell more goods if only they did not have to travel on those winding slopes. He had known many people who had had traffic accidents, some serious, but shrugged this off as a malaise of the late twentieth century – like obesity, breast cancer or Aids, only more widespread.

There was something particularly vicious about travelling by vehicle in Argyll. Maybe it was the natural twists and turns of the routes as they skirted the hills, lochs and rock faces. The roads seemed of poor quality, constantly under repair, and somehow narrow, even where there was plenty of space for a wider gauge. There were precious few alternative modes of transport, however, with a few slow trains creaking over the hills from Glasgow to Oban but bypassing the mountainous land mass of most of Argyll. The economics were sound, of course – with so few people in Cowal, Kintyre or mid-Argyll that Beeching would have closed them all in the 1960s had they ever existed, long before the modernising, prudent government of the 1980s had the chance. There were ferries, of course, but only where the needs were obvious and essential, and there were a few bridges. Common complaints from car travellers alluded to the tortuous routes up one side of a loch only to turn and drive down the other side – all to cover a distance of a few miles as the crow flies. People going about their day-to-day lives and running late would get angry and frustrated by this surreal routine, driving faster and faster. Driving in Argyll was a health hazard.

Robert drove easily but carefully, taking pleasure in Jean's excitement. They were driving to Inveraray where she would meet up with a Royal Navy boat, a training vessel for students and other young people. She had taken to sailing since their move to Argyll and learned sea craft, becoming adept in a short time. Rarely fully satisfied with an inherently selfish pleasure, Jean had helped with the training of young people in an initiative funded by Glasgow University and managed by the Navy. By the end of this planned voyage she was to be a qualified instructor and able to extend her educational role.

'Complementary interests' was a thought going through Robert's mind. He and Jean were suited in sharing passions and activities but not needing to pursue everything in the same way, to the same degree. They genuinely enjoyed the other's pursuits and understood their interest while not always having to be involved. The day before, Robert had sketched all day, an activity most people would suspect of sloth, but not Jean. She had taken on extra domestic and business burdens to allow her husband the free time to draw, seeing his activity as paramount with the running of the shop, tending to the children, singing in the choir, attending a concert of classical music. In their five years in Tarbert, a short visit on the scale applied by local lore, their lives had become seamless and whole. Jean's sailing was as important as Robert's sketching and the couple made no distinction. As they drove that morning, the latest production of Robert's art, an almost finished self-portrait, lay on the back seat of the car.

Rounding a bend, rocks to the left and steep drop to the right, they were confronted by an oncoming van, a large Mercedes, on their side of the road and looking for all the world like a van without a driver. Robert knew instinctively that a pull to the left would result in a certain deadly collision of metal on stone and a head-on collision of the two vehicles, while steering to the right was a hazardous manoeuvre at any time. In the fraction of a second available, he decided the only chance of escape was to cross to the other side of the road, leaving the Mercedes to proceed on the borrowed territory.

Some people in Argyll are not fond of tourists on driving holidays. For some, the reasons are given as low-key grumbling, 'They drive too slowly' or 'Too interested in the views'. Others claim to have had a major fright or actual accident caused by foreign travellers forgetting they should drive on the left. Various stories circulate, offering different versions starring a carload of Swiss, French or Germans zooming at ninety miles per hour up the wrong side of the road, straight towards them, smiling and waving as they do so – a rural equivalent of an urban myth.

The Mercedes was being driven not by a holidaymaker but a working man who had dropped some article and was scrambling to retrieve it from the floor of his cab. It is not known if the driver was hurrying to keep an appointment. It is reasonable to assume that he was late.

Grasping the offending article, the van driver sat up straight in his seat, automatically correcting the direction of his vehicle just as Robert Pine chose the only option in a desperate attempt to avoid him. The result was a crash at high speed, the erring Mercedes smashing into the passenger side of the Pines' car, Jean's side. Jean was badly hurt with extensive damage to the left side of her body and to her head. Robert was cut, bruised and shaken but could walk, talk and think – unlike his wife.

The day took on an air that threatens the grasp of reality by the speed of change, illness and pain, the sudden transformation of a happy time into a time of fear, bringing portents of disaster. The accident happened miles from the nearest town or telephone box, but a seemingly empty road rapidly became a scene of care and concern and in the time that was necessary for help to be summoned, an ambulance was sent spinning up the road. Time ticking by as Jean's smashed and seemingly lifeless body lay and her husband fretted. The two were rushed to hospital in Vale of Leven forty miles away, the nearest major service. Jean had suffered serious head injuries and was shipped out to the

Southern General Hospital, Glasgow. She had not regained consciousness and required emergency surgery and intensive care. Prospects looked bleak for Jean Pine and her husband was advised. In the meantime, his minor injuries required that he be discharged and sent home by ambulance. Robert was sent off, battered and scared, in the opposite direction from his seriously damaged Jean.

By the time Robert was returned to Tarbert, the village knew of the car accident though were thin on facts. The children had found out in all sorts of ways and were terrified, thinking their mother had died. The game of Chinese whispers can be fun and can be vicious; Jean's children were unwitting victims of the latter experience. The oldest of the children, Jackie, had been told in the village hairdressers that her mother had been in a car accident and rushed to hospital in Glasgow, always the worst of signs. Told to telephone the hospital, for four hours Jackie put off the call, suspecting her mother dead and not wanting to be told. Jackie had to try and find some strength for the others, all along wanting to cry for her mother and be with her. The three children felt far away, lost and helpless.

Robert found himself in Tarbert, without car, taxi or train, ninety miles from his wife who might die. He found himself telling the three children of their mother's predicament and feeling their terror and panic. For the first time he doubted his reasons for moving to that place.

Within hours, he had been given a car, the keys to a flat in Glasgow and an undertaking to help with the care of the children. Robert discovered he had friends in Tarbert.

~

Glasgow, Scotland. 1988.
Robert was tidying up the flat before driving the short journey to the hospital. Since the accident, he had spent most of his life going backwards and forwards to the city, spending his days and evenings at Jean's bedside. Jean had been in intensive care for months and experienced life-threatening crises from time to time, appearing as if she would succumb to the lesions on her brain caused by the impact and skull splinters. The left side of her body had been damaged in other ways, severe on their own, but hardly worth a mention compared with the threat posed by the damage to her brain.

For much of those early hospital months, Jean was unconscious and when conscious, speechless. Each visit to her bedside was a long, aching monologue as the visitors, mainly Robert, chatted about day-to-day life back home and all of the patient's familiar and favourite pursuits. No acknowledgement was given, no flicker of interest perceived, as the soliloquies rambled on and on, in those dowdy, chemical-smelling hospital wards. The bleakest days for Robert had been when he did not know if Jean would live and could not know if she heard his tales of Tarbert. The combined pressure was enough to prise the last strands of reality from the most patient, caring individual. Many families ended or reduced their vigils after a week, not through lack of love but through their own grief and the pain of being there, watching the human being settle for an existence without essence. Most families shared the burden among the close adults but Jean and Robert did not have this comfort. Jean's children visited and helped but were too young to carry a major share of the visiting. They would be called on to take up adult responsibilities soon enough. So Robert was more or less alone on these journeys and carried much of the burden of remaining calm through the fear barrier.

Robert's visits to Glasgow were the central focus in his life, taking priority over all else. A few days before the car accident, the Pines had finalised the deal on the sale of Springside Cottage and the purchase of Ashens Cottage. In the West Highlands such matters took a long time, with a lack of competition in housing markets allowing the leisure of careful contemplation and reflection. Robert and Jean thought hard and long about the move, being happy at Springside. They had improved the property and it was in an ideal position to provide bed and breakfast services, a commercial aspect they had not pursued vigorously. Jean had been far more attracted to her work as cook in the Columba Hotel and she had been offered a full-time post which she had agreed to accept. They could take a decent return for their work on Springside, invest some in bringing Ashens up to standard and still have a little contribution to their well-being fund. Jean's salary and the income from the shop would be more than sufficient to support the family.

The children were coming to an age when they were likely to leave home, so space was not crucial. Robert and Jean were concerned about moving out of the village but only a little, having confidence in the strength of their social circles and their own energy in pursuit of the company of others. Ashens Cottage was in a rundown state and required substantial work. A few days before the car accident, the Pine family had moved out of Springside Cottage and into a caravan parked in the grounds of Ashens. A temporary and short-term measure was the intention, until it all went wrong.

Robert had to care for the children, mind the shop, refurbish Ashens Cottage and spend regular time with his wife, languishing in a hospital two hours away by car. His situation was hopeless. Robert's predicament was of the kind which drew sympathetic sighs and little else from people. Others, less caring, produced a certain type of thinly disguised glee at observing the misfortune of neighbours. Since the abolition of public executions, the human desire to witness the downfall of humankind has been relegated to fiction, news broadcasts and gossip. A few people of Tarbert may have responded in that way but most behaved quite differently. They gave Robert the keys to, and sole use of, a flat in Glasgow, the long-term loan of a car and moved in on Ashens – stripping the walls, painting the woodwork, gutting the kitchen, supervising journeymen and grafting themselves. They watched the shop, helped with the children, offered Robert money and time to himself. The good people of Tarbert were different.

Robert had driven down to Glasgow the night before and gone straight to the hospital. The good news was that recent improvement in Jean's health had been sustained. The doctors were now confident she would not die of her injuries, nor would she be left in the immobile, dependent state originally feared. She would need hospital care for months to come and a great deal of social stimulation to orient herself back into her world. Her memory was badly reduced but could improve with time and patience. The medics believed Jean's long-term memory would return first but her short-term recall would take longer, much longer. Robert only heard the good news, being delighted to have his friend and wife back in the conscious world. No time was spent considering the personal loss to Jean – that intelligent, articulate, active and energetic person who had set off for Inveraray early one morning a few months previously. They had all lived too long with the prospect of Jean's death to do anything other than celebrate her survival.

The night before he had stayed late at the hospital holding Jean's hand, chatting, smiling, animated and friendly towards everyone in the ward. There are precious few ways to celebrate with someone still terribly ill, frail and confined to a hospital bed. It was dark when he left the hospital. Winding his way in the car, dipping down into the tunnel burrowing under the River Clyde then veering off left towards the West End of Glasgow, Robert Pine was thinking of his good fortune. Life would be different but all would be well, once again, for Robert and Jean.

Arriving at the flat he prepared for bed, changing into the nightdress he had brought. Not ready for sleep, he sat in an armchair sipping tea and reviewing his scrapbook. There had been some coverage in the newspapers concerning Lady Colin Campbell and controversy on whether she was born a male or a female. The journalist quoted the technical terms before slipping into the salacious nudge-nudging which inevitably accompanied such articles. It had not helped that there had been an acrimonious and scandalous divorce case wherein claim and counter-claim were mounted. Nor had it helped that the woman involved was a sultry and beautiful Jamaican model, married to a titled man. The article read as if only unusual, special people were likely to experience such physiological difficulties and changes. Yet, on other days, the same newspapers carried stories of dustbin men, labourers, salesmen or other miscellaneous Joe Soaps undergoing sex changes. The mass media and the public much preferred the exotic. Robert was used to dismissing the extraneous waffle and learning a little from each piece of journalism. He preferred to think of Lady Colin Campbell as a hermaphrodite, a mystical creature alluded to in ancient mythology, and marvelled at magic come to life.

The next morning he washed breakfast dishes, changed the bedding and folded his clothes away in his overnight bag. Since Jean's hospitalisation he had spent time on his own, the first time in his adult life, and had changed in ways he had not anticipated. Packing his night attire in the bottom of the bag, he felt a twinge of guilt at the brief pleasure he had enjoyed during his periods of solitude while his wife had been in hospital.

~

Carlisle, England. 1989.
The car park was like most car parks though bigger and cleaner than some. Robert had driven from Tarbert, setting out early that morning with Jean and Kirsty and was a little weary though terribly on edge. Jean was still very much in the recup-

eration stage and Kirsty had come along to look after her. During the journey Jean had moments of anger and instability and Robert was thankful for Kirsty's company. Fiona had on many occasions refused to meet Jean and this occasion was no exception. Kirsty would look after Jean while Robert met his children.

'Children', he really had to stop calling them that. They were adults now, with their own lives and their own minds, he hoped. Fiona had made it clear from the beginning that she blamed him for the break-up of her parents' marriage. She had been adamant but Robert kept hoping her experience of life would mellow some of her attitudes. Duncan followed his sister's lead and influence in these matters. He was a quiet and peaceful young man, bright but not as assertive or forthright as his older sister. Robert's life seemed to him to be full of strong-willed women and easy-going men.

This half-way rendezvous had been arranged so that Robert could meet not only his children but his first grandchild. When Fiona had married her German boyfriend, Hacky, in 1987, she refused to allow Robert, her father, to attend her wedding let alone give her away. This had been a terrible hurt and today's meeting was to be the first since that day. Robert was to meet Duncan, Fiona, Hacky and grandson, Alexander. For two precious hours he enjoyed his true parental status and hoped these tentative steps towards reconciliation would lead to many another happy meeting.

Robert wished the children would visit him in Tarbert. So far they had refused all invitations, probably to avoid upsetting their mother – well, Robert hoped that was their reason. He would continue to invite them and see what happened in the future. All too soon he had to say his farewells and watch his children drive away. Uncharacteristically, Robert Pine felt bleak and pessimistic.

~

Ashens Cottage, Tarbert, Argyll. 1990.
Jean's recovery had been slow but evident. Her discharge from hospital had brought palpable relief to all the family but they understood she was still physically fragile and would need years to recover fully. The children were a little distressed to see the changes in Jean. She had been a dynamo, full of ideas and plans,

keeping all of the children on their toes but bringing more pleasure than discipline. Their mother had always known what she wanted and made all the children feel safe, standing up for them first and foremost. Jean was now frail, physically weak and easily fatigued. The only limit on the distress of the children was knowing that Jean was now home and she would get strong again.

Jean was tending to get easily frustrated by small, daily dilemmas. Her concentration and memory were badly affected to the extent that she could not cope with a choice between pairs of socks or radio programmes. Yet Jean still knew who Jean was, her temper flaring up in irritation at her inability to fulfil the minor chores of domesticity and choices of personal preference. The family fretted about their mother's inner turmoil and her physical dependence. Robert worried too but did not display his concern. Instead he did most of the work and took care of his wife as if this were his natural role in life.

~

Out of the pain of Jean's slow recovery came forth the sweetness of husband and wife spending a great deal of time together. The couple blessed the fact they had discovered friendship first, before discovering love, sex and matrimony. The friendship lasted and saw them through those difficult years. They wanted to spend time together, something Jean's recuperation interfered with only occasionally and then never for long.

As the months stretched on, Robert found himself undergoing a reversal of circumstances. Having previously discovered himself on his own for periods and for the first time in his adulthood, he now found himself alone rarely and only for brief periods. The lack of privacy would have been resented by some but not Robert. He was incapable of feeling that way towards Jean who had given him so much and who needed him now. He missed the leisurely strolls, sketch book under arm or time writing his poetry with no other presence, no possibility of distraction. What he realised he could not do without was his time as a woman. As time went on, Robert would set Jean up, making sure all her needs were met, then move himself upstairs to another room, there to put on his favourite dresses, blouses and underwear.

Robert had made no conscious decision to continue wearing

women's clothes but found himself compelled to do so. He was now running more risks of discovery than ever before in his life. Jean was convalescing but was not without mobility, curiosity and a desire to be with her partner. Before long she discovered Robert in his dresses. The initial explanation of humour soon wore thin and, late one night, husband and wife sat down and spoke to each other about each other. For the first time in his life, at sixty years of age, Robert Pine admitted to another human being that he needed to dress as a woman, that part of him felt as a woman.

Jean was his friend, his lover and his wife. She tried to understand Robert's need to wear the clothes made and designed for women. That was all she was asked to think about, wearing women's clothing. Jean understood that Robert enjoyed the dressing up, feeling good and relaxed when he did so. She also understood his peccadillo was unusual and would not be readily comprehended by the children or the villagers. The children were too young to have such a notion explained to them and, besides, they did not have to know. Jean thought that most of the villagers would take flight and conclude that Bob Pine was homosexual, strange, a danger to children, unreliable. Robert was none of those things and so must be protected from those labels as, especially, must the children. After all, she considered her husband's behaviour little more than a harmless eccentricity.

Jean and Robert reached an understanding: he could dress as he wished on two nights each week, only in the privacy of their home and when the children were not around. Campbell, the only child still at home, was out a great deal so secrecy should be easy to achieve. Robert gratefully accepted the arrangement and thanked his gods for bringing him Jean as his wife.

~

Ashens Cottage, Tarbert, Argyll. 1992.
Robert and Jean had their home to themselves, all the children having left on their own adult adventures. Jackie and Kirsty were living with partners in Tarbert while Campbell had gone off to Stirling University. The two young women visited their mother and father, as they had come to know Robert years before, but the distance between Ashens Cottage and Tarbert did not make this a daily routine. More often, Jackie and Kirsty

Robert and Jean ready
to take to the floor,
1981

Robert and
Jean at the
Burns
Federation
Conference in
Irvine, 1981

Robert with his son Duncan, his daughter Fiona and
grandson Alexander, October, 1989

Robert, Jean, Jackie, Kirsty and Campbell at a fancy
dress party (*c*.1983)

Rebecca and Jean at
Ashens Cottage and
(*below*) Kiltie's, Tarbert,
October, 1998
(© Reg McKay)

Again, at Ashens Cottage (© Reg McKay) . . .

. . . and Kiltie's, Tarbert (© Reg McKay)

THIS PAGE AND OPPOSITE: Rebecca enjoying the
spectacular scenery around the village of Tarbert, 1998
(© Reg McKay)

RIGHT AND BELOW:
Rebecca in her Burns
corner in Ashens
Cottage, September,
1998 (© Reg McKay)

would look in on their parents at the shop as Jean would occasionally go along with her husband for the company and a chin wag with local customers. Campbell returned infrequently for a holiday weekend or seasonal break but preferred to stay in Stirling more often than not.

Jean had become stronger and more alert, still with some way to go but unrecognisable compared to her vulnerable state of four years earlier. She had proved her resilience but was determined to improve further. Her major, lasting difficulty was a continuing problem with short-term memory, a spasmodic hitch which infuriated her still. Now and then, serving in the shop, she would have to count the cost of two or three items several times. Sometimes she had to be asked for a *Sunday Times* or *Observer* two or three times, forgetting the order between the request and reaching out to the counter between her and the customer. At other times her memory was fine, adding to Jean's frustration, but a clear signal that she was continuing to heal.

Jean's improving health had resulted in the Pines' gradual return to the social circuit. Sailing was out, of course, and would be forever. The Poetry and Bridge Clubs were gentle pursuits but Jean's card game was struggling to return to her former skill level. They also returned to Scottish country dancing, gently at first but with increasing verve and enthusiasm as Jean's physical strength returned, assisted by the demands of the dance routines. They had returned to their trips to Glasgow or Edinburgh, taking in live concerts of classical music, plays and opera. The couple were cautious about the extra demands on Jean and continued to stay at home more often than they had before the crash.

Jean had grown accustomed to Robert dressed in his feminine outfits. At first she had to adjust, finding a strange and strong difference between these sessions and times before when he would dress up in a frock as part of an outfit for a play or fancy dress party. The knowledge that he was dressing in a frock for its own sake, because he wanted to and no other reason, shook her a little initially. Robert was known to be skilled in designing and manufacturing elaborate and extravagant dresses, flared mini skirts and low-cut tops. All that aptitude had been admirably displayed in the years they had been together but always for dramas or other special social events. Since their compact he had gone through stages of dressing conservatively with only one or two items, then moved on to full ensembles including make-up, tights and underwear. When Robert started to make regular purchases of women's clothes and show these off to his wife, as one does after a day's shopping, Jean had grown a little uneasy. Finally, he started dressing as a woman three or four nights a week, sometimes more often. Jean reassured herself that he had kept the most important part of the bargain in that he only dressed up in the privacy of their home. Then she would be unnerved, not knowing who was to be her companion that night, Robert or that other person he called Susan. That night Jean was feeling fragile about her health, and a little confused and pessimistic about the future. Jean was sitting in the lounge, quiet and preoccupied with her own worries when Susan waltzed in to the room. Susan had been around several times that week though Jean could not remember exactly how many times. Exhausted by the day's efforts and a little exasperated by Susan's unscheduled appearance, Jean looked Robert in the eye, sighed and said, 'For goodness' sake, Robert. Why don't you just go the whole hog!'

The gilt-edged gates of a private paradise opened for Robert Pine with that short sentence. All his life he had had a secret friend called Susan. From time to time, Robert liked to pretend he was Susan and that was all, or so he thought. He had understood the strength of the need as a compulsion, really. Standing in the freezing latrine of an Army barracks in the middle of the night, pyjama bottoms discarded and pulling bloomers over goose-pimpled thighs – all that was more than a game.

If Robert Pine had stopped to consider, he would have realised that it had taken him sixty-two years to find out what he had always known – he wanted to be a woman. He had always wanted to be a woman at every point in his life. Susan was not an imaginary friend, he *was* Susan and always had been Susan. It had taken an off-the-cuff comment from the woman he loved to show him the way. He, the intelligent, articulate, worldly-wise adult had needed the approbation of this other person, the woman he loved. Robert had the truth now and he would not let it go. That night, exhilarated, he could not sleep.

Jean had noticed nothing unusual in Robert that night. He had gone a little quiet after she had put him down in her gentle manner. He was sensitive to her moods and had taken such care of her over the past four years. She considered herself to be a lucky woman, having Robert to see her through her injuries and putting up with her demands. She counted her blessings to herself but still could not relax, could not sleep. Jean felt a pressure push inside her chest like a feeling of dread or some portent of doom.

13 Enigma Variations

. . . to weave my crazy path 'gainst all the odds,
a thing of insignificance among the Gods.
REBECCA PINE IN 'THE SACRED FLAME'

The Cottage, West Loch, Tarbert, Argyll. 1992.
On November nights, the loch shone black and liquid, increasing its threat of a cold drowning. Clouds would come over low as if they had skimmed the tips of waves on the open sea and, hitting land, raised themselves to their rightful height, but reluctant and languid. The climate after dark brought a grinding, seductive sleaziness best hidden from or celebrated but ignored at peril.

The Cottage bobbed with pliant shadows cast from the flickering heat of burning logs and licking tongues of candles. The lone figure reclined on the fleshy crushed leather of a settle, bulbous brandy glass cupped in hands, pulled to her face, shielding her from pernicious amber heat. As she looked out through lashing branches, frantic in the gusts, a time and place was called up:

The wind blew as 'twad blawn its last;
The rattling showers rose on the blast;
The speedy gleams the darkness swallow'd;
Loud, deep, and lang the thunder bellow'd:
That night, a child might understand,
The Deil had business on his hand.

'The ponce! Coming up here with his airs and graces pretending to be super-normal like some missionary come to quell the peasants and teach them better ways. The error of their ways. Ha! You've gone native, haven't you? You and your clubs and dances and poxy poetry.'

In the background, orchestral music swelled to a false peak

only to subside to low, threatening rumbles. A sip of the brandy and a cold stare down over the path, watching the rising waters through the thrashing branches of a rowan tree and new words came to mind:

Warlocks and witches in a dance:
Nae cotillon, brent new frae France,
But hornpipes, jigs, strathspeys, and reels,
Put life and mettle in their heels.
A winnock-bunker in the east,
There sat auld Nick, in shape o' beast . . .

'You an' your jigging, Bob Pine. You think we don't know what you're at, eh? What you're really like. Pfff . . .'

The background music twisted and turned, first almost inaudible then a swelling false crescendo. The music disturbed many people but was Newman's favourite piece for relaxation and reflection. Wherever she went she would have a copy of Elgar's *Enigma Variations* – at home on vinyl, a tape cassette in her car and here on CD. Years before, Newman had been introduced to the music by an older man, met by mistake, common thoughts discovered by accident and with surprise. He had been to public school, Cambridge, and came from a background wherein classical music, Latin quotations and the ability to recite long screeds of obscure poetry had been second nature. Newman had barely achieved a Leaving Certificate, had no job, was twenty-two years old and had no plans. Still they had met and spent long nights drinking whisky-spiked chicory coffee, exploring the meaning of life and the frailty of human nature while listening to Elgar, always Elgar. The older man had taught and taken, leaving Newman's life suddenly and without warning. On that blustery November night by West Loch, he had crept into her thoughts at first fondly then with the rising, bitter sap of resentment.

Newman's friend had been in the limelight and highly respected, while deemed to be capable, honest and trustworthy. A very public family man, he had provided a safe and reassuring model of behaviour. A stable influence on all during a time of great change, he was frequently invited to make speeches, write papers and was often interviewed by the Press. In the 1950s, the advent of television was beginning to have an impact and her friend was shaping up as one of the main beneficiaries. His handsome, honest face and velvet, dulcet tones fitted the bill.

In the early hours sitting by Newman's side on that threadbare, lumpy settee in the cramped bedsit, he had confessed all. Newman had heard him out, to a soundtrack of Elgar. The sham of his life and marriage was described without acrimony but with measured, descriptive sadness within a lament of self-imposed discipline and denial. No more the paragon of virtues but the wounded, misunderstood victim, his peeling revelations shifted the power in the room to a balance of equality, calling for generosity from cautious young Newman. As starlings awoke and thick-bottomed, glass milk bottles chinked together before thudding on doorsteps, Newman was awakened. The raised arm of the Dansette forced Elgar to play on, one side of the vinyl forced to repeat and return, repeat and return.

A secret life fuelled by discovery, painted the colour of pathos, serenaded by Elgar and confined to that single city room. Every night for three months then no more. No word, no letter, no final visit, just an end and no more.

The memories left Newman angry and lonely. She had cursed her work, spat invective at the villagers and wished Tarbert to slide into the sea. As ever, her final thoughts returned to Bob Pine as a primeval emotion emerged and jealousy flamed the melancholy aches of old.

Swallowing a draught of brandy-spiked vitriol, Newman stared out at West Loch and swore an oath: 'I'm going to hurt you, Bob Pine. See if I don't.'

14 I Did Not Choose

I did not choose the body of a man
Nor did those loving parents specify
To that high architect who drew my plan . . .
REBECCA PINE IN 'I DID NOT CHOOSE'

The Surgery, Tarbert, Argyll. 1993.
You can tell a great deal about how an organisation is run by
the range of magazines in the waiting room; at least Robert Pine
thought so. In the surgery, the reading material was derived
from a large pile of women's magazines, some very recent.
Where did they come from – the reception staff, the nurse, Dr
Macdonald's wife, donations from the public? Robert browsed
an article on ritualistic female circumcision and skimmed the
fashion pages. All very fine to while away a few minutes but not
his type of reading at all, much preferring weightier tomes and
more challenging prose.

Everyone passing through the waiting room knew everyone
else passing through the waiting room, and by first names. So
familiar were many of the villagers that they could predict, with
reasonable accuracy and sometimes certainty, why others were
calling on the doctor. The victims of chronic or recurring
complaints were well known, while those signed off work and
seeking another line were usually easy to predict. Those to
whom illness was a stranger were often open about their
misfortune and happy to provide florid descriptions of each
symptom to any neighbour, lest the malaise should visit them or
their family. The surgery's waiting area was a favourite venue
for the swapping of medical histories and information on the
current outbreak of colds, influenza or the generic virus.
Nobody seemed to have children who picked up head lice in the
playground, wives with addiction problems or husbands with
prostate cancer. As patients came and went, chatting all the

while, Robert was polite and friendly but gave no hint as to why he had booked a consultation with Dr Macdonald. 'It will be the virus then,' his neighbours would conclude.

Neil Macdonald was well respected as a general practitioner. Originating from the islands, he had settled in Tarbert many years before and had served as the village doctor ever since, though fast approaching retirement age by 1993. While locum doctors would serve placements at the surgery now and then, Neil Macdonald was the mainstay of health care, night and day, all week and every week. As a doctor, Neil had come to know everyone in the village and farther afield throughout the scattering of isolated houses and farmsteads in the surrounding countryside. He had attended births, deaths and every other life crisis in-between. He had called in the middle of the night to alleviate pain and soothe away fear. He had given the worst of news and the best of news. He had reassured the low of spirit and cajoled those consuming too many spirits. Every family in Tarbert owed a personal debt to Dr Neil Macdonald.

Neil and his wife were also villagers and lived their life in Tarbert to the full. They were involved in yachting, the Gaelic choir, community politics and every fund raiser for every good addition to the welfare of the villagers. Neil was a particularly fine singer, had appeared at the Mod and could often be found at Burns Suppers toasting the lassies or singing solo. Ever adaptable, he had joined in a local Barber Shop group along with Robert Pine. Dr and Mrs Macdonald could also be found in local hotels or pubs, out for dinner or simply partaking of a dram and choosing to share the extended company of others. More often than not, standing at the corner of the bar, glass in hand, Neil Macdonald would smoke a cigarette or two. Like all doctors, he was human with human tastes and in Tarbert such tastes could not be concealed. Dr Macdonald did not try to hide his weaknesses and the folk of Tarbert trusted him all the more.

Robert's appointment had been made after a great deal of thought and consideration. He was not in the habit of rushing to the doctor with every little ailment or niggle. Unlike the new moral majority of the nineties who demanded constant good health and expected longevity to boot, Robert understood that to be human meant being unwell at times. He would most often treat ill health by the self-administration of an aspirin or an early night. Four extra hours' sleep were of no value to him on this occasion.

Robert had gone to Dr Macdonald to tell him that he wanted to change sex, to become a woman. Since the night of Jean's tired and careless remark, changing gender had been his sole preoccupation. He had wanted to rush to the doctor the next day but had hesitated a short while. He had no doubt, no doubt at all about his wishes but had to discuss this further with Jean and reflect on the best way forward. His scrapbook told him enough about the procedure to know that the first approach had to be made to a doctor. The local general practitioner was the gateway to other, specialist medical services. Robert did not bother thinking about other doctors in other towns or cities. He saw no reason why he should not approach Neil Macdonald, in his little surgery in the little village. He trusted Neil and that was that.

Robert also knew Neil Macdonald socially through singing, the choir and dancing. Jean had become particularly close to Mrs Macdonald through sailing and just gelling as two people who enjoyed each other's company. Where others may have seen complications, Robert perceived no problem. Once decided that he should go to the next, medical stage he had popped into the surgery and made an appointment with his doctor and his neighbour.

Robert suspected that Dr Macdonald had not been approached by any other patient regarding a sex change that morning. Nevertheless, the general practitioner did not blink or hesitate, proving supportive and professional throughout. He listened to his patient describe his lifelong need to be a woman and passed no judgement, spoken or unspoken. The consultation ended with the doctor explaining the process whereby he would now refer the matter to the Argyll and Bute Hospital and a psychiatrist would be allocated. The good doctor also prepared Robert for what would be a demanding, intrusive and lengthy process. The concluding farewells included best wishes and an open invitation to return any time he so desired.

Robert Pine would soon be sixty-three years old and he had discussed his lifelong need to be a woman for the second time, with a second person. He had started a train of events which would stop only if he retracted his request and stated that he was happy as a man.

~

Lochgilphead, Argyll. 1994.

The mythology about psychiatrists is that they are as mad as their patients. The conundrum is whether mad doctors choose psychiatry or start sane and grow to be like their patients. As with most myths, there is an iota of truth, expanded numerous-fold to support the original stereotype.

Dr Allan McCulloch did not dress in the staid, grey suits of the physician, preferring bright, unco-ordinated colours in his wardrobe of casual clothes. He was known to speak his mind and managed to make the most outrageous statements sound cheeky and humorous rather than aggressive and slanderous. Passing McCulloch in a hospital corridor, colleagues were no longer surprised to be greeted with a spontaneous outburst of song. Dr McCulloch was at worst eccentric and at best respected by many grateful patients, including Robert Pine.

By 1993, psychiatry had long since ceased to be a concern with therapy, counselling or helping people to change their lives. Psychiatry had become obsessed with drugs, assessment and avoiding the admission to hospital of ill people. A successful request for a sex change ultimately led to drugs, the operating table, more drugs, then nothing – the ideal of the modern medical model. To get there, the patient had to convince a raft of people of their serious intentions, their merit and, above all, reassure them that they would never change their mind. This cannot be achieved by drugs but requires the applicant to meet and talk with psychiatrists.

Dr McCulloch was good at talking with people. The psychiatrist had a collusive approach, allowing Robert to feel they were on the same side, on the same level and had to work through this together. McCulloch was the gateway to others, crucial in obtaining the required authority. So, he explained the background and purpose to the visit from the peripatetic psychiatrist, the specialist in Edinburgh, the community psychiatric nurse calling on Jean and her appointment to meet with McCulloch himself. All in all, Robert felt edified and included, if a little frustrated by the red tape and the time taken.

Robert Pine was sixty-three years of age and had spoken with six people regarding his lifelong wish to be a woman. He had no way of knowing, but for him the tide was moving rapidly.

~

A83 road north of Tarbert, Argyll. 1994.

The afternoon was chilly and rain looked imminent. Jean Pine did not notice the weather, the road, the trees or the cars speeding past. Jean was walking and thinking with no room left for the mundane demonstrations of the surrounding environment, usually a great source of joy.

Over the previous months, life had run too fast for Jean and she was unsure what would happen next. She and Robert shared everything and spoke about it all but she was still left feeling that everything had run away from her, faster and faster. The community psychiatric nurse had visited that day and their discussion had helped but nothing could take away the sense that her life had changed inexplicably. Nobody, no matter how sympathetic and understanding, could own her life or be her, Mrs Jean Pine, Robert Pine's wife. She understood Robert's need, loved and supported him but still she had not sought this, had not considered this till now. Jean accepted that it was right for Robert to pursue the change but was confused about what was right for her, Jean Pine, Robert Pine's wife.

Jean kept walking and thinking. She would not find an answer to her questions that day.

~

Tarbert, Argyll. 1994.

The three young adults met together now and then but not too often, in the manner of those with their own, full lives to lead. Jackie and Kirsty had flats in the village and that night they were in the older sister's home, having being asked to congregate there by Bob Pine. They shared a sense of awe and foreboding and chatted nervously as they waited for the man they knew as 'Father' to arrive. Campbell tried to crack jokes about what Bob wanted from them and the laughter elicited resulted from anxiety more than the quality of his stand-up routine. They had never before been cited to a meeting with Bob.

Robert Pine arrived alone and later than planned. The young adults could tell that he was as much on edge as they felt. They knew Bob as eloquent, relaxed and loquacious while seldom hesitant or reticent. They all, independently and immediately, worried about their mother. As Bob started his spiel, they expected to be told that Jean's health had taken a turn for the worse, that the prognosis had been wrong and she was seriously ill. The three young adults, children again, fretted about their mother as Robert Pine explained to them his wish to be a woman. Jackie was recalling the feeling of dread she felt that day when told her mother was hurt and she should telephone the hospital. She relived the panic in her chest, her constricted throat and her stomach dropping and pumping, dropping and pumping. All the while Bob Pine was talking of how he had always felt truly female.

As Robert's announcement finally became clear, he paused and waited for a response. Receiving none, he went on to explain that he was seeing a psychiatrist and hoped to have a sex change operation. At some point he would have to dress as a woman and live as such for at least a year before the operation. Still receiving little response, he looked around at the familiar though stunned young faces and reassured them that their mother would be okay, that she knew everything and they would continue to live together.

The living room in Jackie's flat suddenly seemed small and claustrophobic. A tense charge had eclipsed the atmosphere. The young people could not take in what they had been told and were incapable of enquiry. Robert felt he had taken the responsible step of giving Jean's children their place, giving them information, an explanation and an opportunity to ask questions.

Robert Pine left the flat believing his journey had moved on a stage. Back in the lounge three young people were trying to comprehend what they had been told.

~

Kiltie's Shop, Tarbert, Argyll. 1994.
The early-morning frost, mild in the October of Argyll, was beginning to lift Newman's hangover. The frost and the double helping of paracetamol combined to clear her head. Driving into the village she passed the Church of Scotland, inspirational in its austerity, perched high above the road as a warning to all who forgot to enter. The Protestant design was faultless, in Newman's view, declaring both the church's solidity and omniscience. Almost a mirror of the people of these parts – hard as rock and all-knowing.

Newman had continued to feel bitter and angry towards the West Coast Highlanders whom, she believed, had decided to isolate her and refused to befriend her, as if in some unspoken conspiracy. She had tried to fit in as best she could. Compared to her usual behaviour she had been downright sociable, going out of her way to greet known faces and pass comment on the weather or whatever, receiving little change in return. She had intended to join in with more community activities but it had proved difficult with her visits to the village being limited to infrequent weekends. The *Argyllshire Advertiser*, or the *Squeak*, as local papers everywhere are known, was sent regularly to her home by arrangement. The newspaper was full of Brownies' events, farming or fishing information, Council business and the most antiquated form of advertising she had come across. The most informative page of the *Squeak* had letters from the public but even those tended to be simple letters of complaint or self-interest. The sole consolation was that the newspaper took barely two minutes to read, slowly.

When Newman arrived at the Cottage it was usually late on a Friday night after a long week's writing, interviewing, research and general hassle. The drive up did not get any easier, as she sat hunched and expectant over the steering wheel, waiting for the deer to dash out on to the road. She arrived in Tarbert crabby and tired, seeking solace in alcohol. So she was drinking heavily from Friday to Sunday and would return to the city on Monday looking worse for wear than when she had departed for the weekend break. 'Not the point at all. This was not the plan,' she would mutter to herself, staggering to bed, drunk and alone.

Hangover or not, Newman could not do without the Sunday newspapers. One of the glossy supplements had accepted a feature from her some months ago and could be published at any time. The editors were notorious at forgetting all about the freelance writers as soon as they had possession of the articles. Newman had already been paid handsomely for her work and told to watch out in early or late October, an added incentive to her essential ritual of reading all of the Sundays anyway. There was only one place in Tarbert to buy the Sunday newspapers – Kiltie's – and from the proprietor, Bob Pine. Newman enjoyed the voyeur's pleasure of knowing Bob Pine without Bob Pine knowing her or showing any flicker of interest or memory. Then again, he was unlikely to remember her with all the change she had endured.

Kiltie's had its usual Sunday customers. Locals slipping in for a

Sunday Post, twenty Club and Irn Bru to quell the self-administered dehydration left from the night before; visitors walking down from yachts moored at the pontoon, buying the heavy papers, tea bags, bacon, milk and sometimes Irn Bru for the very same reason as the locals.

Bob Pine served Newman with the polite and engaging manner she found so infuriating in this man but welcome in others. Standing in the shop, completing the minor transaction, she often acknowledged that of all the Tarbert residents, he was the one, the only one, who made overtures of friendship. His courtesy, of course, infuriated Newman even more. Without being asked, Robert placed Newman's thick bundle of newspapers in a carrier bag, recycled from the Co-operative store in the village, counted the change out on to the customer's palm and wished her a good day in improved weather. By the time Newman was walking to her car, the hangover was threatening to return, a pulse throbbing at her temple.

Back at the Cottage Newman poured coffee from the percolator, bubbling and hissing in the kitchen, and sat down to serve her fix of newsprint. As she flicked through the bundle searching for the magazines, discarding the unwanted and irritating advertising blurb, she discovered a one-page letter in handwriting she recalled from notes on a drama, decades earlier. Leaning back into the comfort of the armchair, Newman swallowed strong, hot coffee and, lighting her first cigar of the day, started to read the letter:

Dear Customer,

Thank you for shopping at Kiltie's today and over a period of time.

In the eleven or twelve years we have been here in Tarbert there have been many changes in the village, and we, too, have made a number of small changes in the shop, always with a view to giving you a better service.

Jean has, of course, had a great deal to contend with since her terrible injuries six years ago and it is largely due to the support of the village that she has made continuous strides in her recovery.

You will shortly see another change at Kiltie's and one for which we hope to receive your continuing support. This change affects me personally. Over many years – indeed since my earliest recollection – I have truly felt myself to be female rather than male, but old-fashioned conventions have kept me from showing my true self. Now, however, with medical and psychiatric help, I am setting out on a course which will hopefully result in a modern-day sex change. A necessary part of the process is that I dress and live as a woman – which I shall be doing permanently in just a few days' time.

Jean and I will continue to live and work harmoniously together, and we hope you will continue to accept our best service from Kiltie's. Henceforth, however, I shall no longer be known as Bob but as –

Rebecca Pine.

'Well, well! Now they'll get you, Bob Pine. You're for it now.' Newman placed the letter on her knee and looked out to the loch, staring westwards away from Tarbert, Kiltie's and Robert Pine. Her eyes looked glazed as if tears were imminent, but whether through sadness or mirth was not evident. Rubbing her chin and smacking her lips in a medley of tics which she always did as she spotted a plot or grasped a theme, Newman reached for the telephone and started dialling.

～

Ashens Cottage, Tarbert, Argyll. 1994.

Jean and Robert agreed that the medical and psychiatric staff served them both well with the right level of support and factual information. Facts such as Robert's requirement to dress as a woman for a year as part of the proof establishing his determination to be a woman. This information influenced their understanding of a range of implications, such as: the time to be taken before the operation; the public's knowledge of a private affair; Robert waking, working, playing and sleeping as a woman; Jean living with Robert waking, working, playing and sleeping as a woman; and more. All of this would occur in Tarbert, unless the couple chose to go and live elsewhere.

The medical profession had different views on this dilemma. Some would recommend emigration to a community where no one knew the man and populace in order to avoid embarrassing accusations or protestations. This school thought that living among people was difficult enough, particularly as the man learned to wear a wig, walk in heels and sit down while wearing a skirt. The opposing school thought the only aspect of life which should change was the man's attire and name, everything else in his life remaining – this school was suspicious that all people are capable of acting in a completely different way when surrounded by strangers. Whether or not any of the advocates of this school had ever lived in a village of a few hundred souls is not known. Nor is it known if in living in such a small community they had made personal changes any more profound than, say, the colour of their hair, the car they drove or the length of their skirts.

Robert and Jean had little patience with such debates, believing they had chosen Tarbert for good reasons which remained the same good reasons. They belonged in Tarbert. In Tarbert they were among friends. Robert and Jean were staying put.

The procedure, as Robert understood it, required him to wait for his psychiatrist to invite him to adopt the public persona of a woman. He had to wait for a green flag which would be signalled when his talking therapy had somehow reached the right stage. In short, someone else would suggest that he was ready to dress and be known as a woman. Robert decided that he knew his own mind best of all and he had been ready to be a woman for nigh on sixty-four years. Jean understood that Robert was certain of his wish to be female and had never been more sure of anything in his life. It was agreed: they would continue their lives in the village as before and Robert would dress and be known as a woman.

Robert Pine had struggled to consider a name, his new name. Throughout his life he had thought of, and as, Susan. The most natural development would be for him to take on that name, to be Susan publicly as he had privately for so long. Practical problems would ensue, however, such as the number of documents referring to him as RJP or R.J. Pine – Robert John Pine. His signature, his drawings and poetry. The list went on and was proving to be more of a hindrance to Robert than his initial excitement at the prospect of choosing a woman's name. It would be more convenient if his new name had the same initials as his old name, the name he was to discard. He did not want to make the same mistake as others, reaching out for any old female name starting with the right letters. Robert did not want a name that was merely convenient or the female alternative to his given name – Roberta, Bobby. Or worse, a name so extreme in its representation it did not suit him at all – Toyah, Joy, Samantha, Trixie. His new name marked a renaissance and must resound with the femininity of his true nature while feeling right for him, leaving no one in doubt about who he really was and who she was to become.

As if these dilemmas were not a sufficiently heavy burden, Robert Pine could not just decide his new name but would have to do so legally. On 10 October 1994, he attended an appointment with Alan George Taylor Walker, Notary Public, Campbeltown. In the presence of the solicitor, Robert John Pine signed a solemn declaration by virtue of Section 17 of the Statutory Declarations Act 1835. He was required to swear: 'In the light of medical and psychiatric treatment which I am undertaking with the purpose of effecting a change of sex I wish, from this date, to be known as Ms Rebecca Jane Pine.'

A few days later, Rebecca told the world her real name.

~

Stonefield Castle Hotel, Tarbert, Argyll. October, 1994.
While being a beautiful part of the world, Tarbert was no sleepy dormitory. The traditional industries had taken a hammering here as elsewhere but work persisted and people lived in the village to make a living as well as to appreciate their environment. A good number of fishing boats remained, fish farming had taken off, sheep and deer grazing were everywhere. The recent developments in agricultural and fishing production had beneficial side effects in that it had become easy to buy venison, smoked salmon, scallops or oysters, all produced by local entrepreneurs employing local people.

Then there was tourism: the vicinity was popular with those travelling by car, hitch-hiking, motorcycle and even bicycle. The sheltered cove of the harbour made Tarbert a major yachting centre with a range of concomitant services – ship's chandlers, sail makers, nautical engineers and purveyors of equipment and provisions. Britain's second-largest yacht race series next to Cowes was based there, bringing an armada of competitive yachts, race followers, fun seekers and thousands of people for an early start to the summer. A music festival ran for a week and a similar surge in the population occurred, this time bringing folk singers, leather-clad blues bands, spaced-out rock guitarists, spoof acts, choirs from Trinidad, traditional fiddlers, steel bands, massed drummers and flag wavers, professionals, amateurs, groupies and work.

The local services responded with a type of social schizophrenia. During the busy season some shops would triple their stock, their staff and their opening hours while others made no effort, more content to take the extra profit for the same effort. Most of the public houses stayed as they were, happy to cater for the raucous hordes of drunken crews, the wilder nights of music and to specialise in lock-ins, allowing the drinking and spending to continue to sunrise. During these festivals, night-time Tarbert took on the air and mores of a bacchanalian orgy, for many young people at least.

Other establishments changed, catching up with the higher expectations of most of the wider world and bringing standards which would receive plaudits anywhere, anytime. The Victoria Hotel had been transformed from a traditional hovel to a welcoming place where strangers felt secure, drinking fine wines and eating the best of local fare. The inside of the bar had been gutted and emerged as a place of soft wood, brass fittings and picture after picture of famous yachts and other vessels. Across the harbour a husband-and-wife team had opened the Anchorage, a small restaurant presenting such exquisite menus that in a city it would be exclusive, with reservations required weeks in advance.

Other hotels, such as the Columba or Stonefield Castle, concentrated on enhancing their traditional standards and approach. During the quiet autumn and winter seasons they would maintain their business by catering for Rotary Club dinners, wedding receptions and other large parties. This resulted in sporadic peaks of demand when the staffing levels had to be increased for one night at a time. Work was available waiting on table, dish washing and cleaning for those willing to take on that type of work for the wages paid.

Jackie and Kirsty worked in the local hotels as waitresses from time to time. It was Saturday night and Jackie was being driven to the Stonefield Castle by the manager when she found out about Robert's letter to the public. For whatever reason – too busy with her young daughter, a day in the house covering domestic chores – she was one of the few villagers who had not heard that morning of Robert's announcement. Such was the level of local scandal that neighbours, usually open and friendly towards the young woman, probably felt too unsure of their own feelings to have the confidence to speak with her that day.

'Bob Pine. Kiltie. The man is going to change to a woman! You read of these things happening elsewhere but not here in Tarbert. Poor Jean. Oh, what will the lassies think of it all!' was the type of more sympathetic reaction expected that day. The villagers would take time to get used to the news. As Jackie was being driven to work, the Tarbert folk had only known for a few hours. Too soon to talk openly with the family, far too soon.

The manager of the Stonefield was gentle and kind. Jackie's shock told him all he needed to know and he was concerned for the young woman. All of his staff and most of his customers were speaking about Robert Pine. Both Jackie and Kirsty were to be working at the hotel that evening and he was concerned at how they would cope. He needed all the staff to work that night or there would be chaos in the serving of meals. Laying aside that pressure, he made a friend for life by making it clear to Jackie that her needs came first and he would understand if she had to go home, see her mother her father, or whatever.

At the hotel, Jackie and Kirsty were given time to themselves. The meeting with Robert in Jackie's house that night was not on their minds. It felt as if they had been told nothing. That Sunday night at the Stonefield Castle they felt angry, let down and betrayed.

Jackie looked around at the faces of the staff and knew that their sole topic of conversation was Bob Pine, father to her, Kirsty and Campbell. It had not been easy settling into Tarbert at first. At school they had called her an English snob because of her accent and where the family lived. She had battled through all that and was part of the local community now, raising a child who belonged to Tarbert. She thought of her own young daughter and wondered when the cruel teasing and jibes would begin. That Saturday night Jackie thought her life had changed for ever.

～

Kiltie's, Tarbert, Argyll. October, 1994.
Argyll had more than its fair share of writers and photographers. Not just the brilliant light of Iain Crichton Smith but writers of children's tales, travelogues, academic tomes, poetry, cookery books and newspaper columns. Not just holiday

snappers but photographers of mountains, lochs, lakes, erotica, daily life and wildlife. Argyll also had visitors, preferring to explore their own countryside over sunning themselves on a Spanish beach or drinking rum at a Caribbean bar. The out-of-season visitors carried with them a sense of connection with the aesthetics of the Highlands and displayed it through hillwalking, rambling, yachting or some creative pursuit. They were often people living in cities, subjecting themselves to the most acute pressure just to earn an income and escape to the country for occasional rest and recuperation.

It did not surprise Robert and Jean that on the day of his announcement, a press photographer had been staying over in the village. Nor was it a shock when he called at the shop and requested permission to take pictures with the intent of publication.

Argyll had its fair share of ringers – people who contact the national press with tips on possible newsworthy stories, and are rewarded for their successful efforts. There was little national interest in the politics, economics or personalities of Argyll, what little interest there was being covered effectively by the commentators based in the central belt. As a result, telephone calls were made on personal issues, scandals and rumours either to the tabloids or gossip columns. There is always interest in people teetering off the rails, being caught in compromising situations or the unusual. Somehow, the setting of the West Highlands added a dimension to stories of everyday life everywhere, as if what is commonplace in the city is somehow more decadent, more salacious and more outrageous in the country.

Robert and Jean were not surprised when their telephone started to ring incessantly. For days, they were bombarded by requests for information, quotes or interviews from every newspaper and magazine in the land. They coped patiently with the pressure though it rocked Jean's continuing physical fragility and her labile emotions. The reporters wanted to know why Robert had made this decision and what Jean intended to do. Time after time, Robert advised that he had always felt truly female. Jean repeated, again and again, that she had had difficulties in coming to terms with his wishes but she loved her husband and would stay with him as long as he wanted. The couple were required to explain how they could stay together. The unspoken assumptions of many of the media people were that sex must have some greater importance than love. Robert and Jean knew what love meant.

The Pines assumed that the press photographer had alerted the newspapers. Some villagers assumed that particular neighbours had made the calls in search of a tips fee. In the Cottage at West Loch, Newman was still on the telephone.

~

Tarbert, Argyll. 1994.
Letters kept arriving at Ashens Cottage. Now they came from farther afield, sometimes from people describing themselves as transgendered, sometimes from couples who had survived the same experiences as Rebecca and Jean but mostly from ordinary people, taking the time to commit to writing how much they supported the Pines' openness and wishing them luck. Occasionally the scribe would describe Rebecca's intentions as wrong or sinful but would do so gently, sympathetically. No hate mail arrived, none at all.

The interest from the media took a wider turn with *The Big Breakfast* show endeavouring to entice an interview, promising 'sensitivity and compassion' and news services offering Jean small fees for articles which would be sold on to a range of publications. Researchers from a Scottish university approached Rebecca, significantly as part of a Media Studies project rather than focusing on gender issues, psychological, sociological or even socio-medical matters. The public reaction and the press interest had achieved a life of its own. Just as suddenly as the birth was the death, with interest coming to an abrupt and unexplained halt. Rebecca and Jean had had their fifteen minutes of fame and survived it well and whole.

In the weeks after Rebecca's public announcement the couple had made an effort to ensure that their friends, family, numerous clubs and societies were advised by them directly rather than hearing the gossip through the grapevine. Letters were dispatched to those living far away such as Tina, Fiona, Duncan and Geoff Ash. Rebecca also wrote to her more distant relatives, such as cousins. The Pines waited for responses, uncertain what to expect.

Of their local clubs, they were advised that a member of the Tarbert Scottish Country Dance Club had taken exception at Bob Pine appearing in their midst dressed as a woman and calling himself Rebecca. Jean and Rebecca were informed of this with great hesitance and regret but, nevertheless, the matter had to be addressed. Had the objector expected the Pines to wither in embarrassment and shame, wilting quietly into the background, they clearly did not know Rebecca and Jean very well. The objector also lacked any comprehension of the heart-searching and determination required before Rebecca started her journey. The Pines were not about to be shaken off now and were not about to concede such decisions and be relegated to secrecy. The objection was against *Rebecca*: Jean would still be welcome as indeed would Bob Pine. Rebecca simply asked for her constitutional rights to be applied and a straightforward vote be taken among the membership, a simple task due to the sparse numbers involved.

While unabashed by her situation, this local difficulty cast an omen on Rebecca's social confidence though not on her resolve. Waiting for the mechanism of the vote, the Pines got on with their lives. They showed up at the Lochgilphead Bridge Club with the suspicion that this may be their last attendance. Local mythology and competitiveness held Lochgilphead people to be strait-laced, conservative and narrow-minded while, by comparison, Tarbert was considered to be bohemian, decadent and easy-going. Rebecca and Jean could only fear the worst.

Robert attended, dressed as Bob Pine and being the Bob Pine other players had come to know. During an interlude in the proceedings, he stood up and asked if he could speak to the group, having an announcement he would like them all to hear. He explained his intentions to be Rebecca and offered the group the opportunity to exclude him, if that was what they wished. Barely had he finished his short speech and returned to his seat, when the response was loud, unanimous and a great relief. The good people of the Lochgilphead Bridge Club had no problems with Robert's plans, applauded his openness and wished him well. Rebecca and Jean Pine would be every bit as welcome to play bridge as Bob and Jean Pine had been. 'Enough said, let's get on with the next rubber,' was the dominant attitude of club members.

That was the beginning and the end of the matter, with members confiding later that they had thought something was going on in Robert's life for some time. Others candidly admitted that they had heard such rumours long before the official announcement. On the way home that night, Robert and Jean expressed their admiration for the effectiveness of human curiosity and communication. They also acknowledged that had they been excluded, the Bridge Club would have struggled to make up the numbers. Perhaps the members' level of human understanding had been enhanced by the greater need to sustain their games of bridge. Robert chortled to himself and thought that was exactly the type of prioritisation he sought. The evening had been good for the Pines and another decision had been made: the world clearly knew about Rebecca so Robert would not be seen in public again.

Rebecca and Jean travelled about Argyll and beyond, pursuing their interests as before with total acceptance. The vote for the Tarbert Scottish Country Dance Club was announced as a tied vote. More than a little hurt at the ambivalence of this group, Rebecca and Jean advised their neighbours they would henceforth resign from the club since they did not wish to offend or upset anyone. Some stalwarts followed the Pines by announcing their resignation and the club's reduced membership began to teeter on the verge of disbanding. As word spread in the tight but extensive world of folk dancing, the letters started again from far and wide, condemning the narrow-minded few of the Tarbert Scottish Country Dance Club.

Responses from family and friends were varied. Tina, as ever, was about to go off on a trip, this time to Mexico and Guatemala following the trail of the Mayan Indians – her retirement seeming more full of exotic adventure than those of half her age. She still took the time to write and admitted to struggling to see her brother as anything other than male. Nevertheless, she would get used to the prospect of having a sister, given time.

Fiona and Duncan were lost to their father now: this change was the final straw. Robert had held on to his dream to be reconciled with his children and his grandchildren in spite of the lack of positive signs. The first and last time he had seen his first grandchild had been in that car park in Carlisle. It now appeared that Rebecca would never have the pleasure of meeting her beloved family nor would her family have the satisfaction of knowing the real person that was to be Rebecca Pine.

As for the cousins and more distant relatives, they tended to reply politely and no more. Robert Pine had formed a closer relationship with some of these good people over the few preceding years but now suspected that they could not cope with his change.

It was beginning to look as if, with the exception of Tina, Rebecca and Jean Pine would have to rely on their recently made friends, those they shared interests with and their supportive neighbours, the people of Tarbert. Rebecca and Jean had chosen their community well but were mourning the lack of acceptance in those from their earlier lives, who had known them for longest. Then a special delivery was made to Ashens Cottage. Addressed to 'Ms R. Pine' was a case of fine wine and a note from an old, old friend – Geoff Ash.

15 None So Pretty

You must try not to mind growing up into a pretty woman.

JANE AUSTEN IN 'EMMA'

Inveraray Castle, Argyll. 18 November, 1994.

Rebecca and Jean Pine had been invited by the Duchess of Argyll to attend a Scottish Country Dance at Inveraray Castle. The Duchess was the patron of cancer charities and the event was to raise funds. Rebecca and Jean had been invited together with other leading lights of Scottish Country Dancing in Argyll and farther afield. The invitation was a delight to the couple who had no hesitation in deciding to be in attendance.

Rebecca had been in the world for five weeks only. They had been awkward weeks, starting with publicity lasting for a full seven days and attracting front-page coverage in many newspapers. The first week had taken on the blur of a restless dream when everything seems somehow slow and strange, not quite real but happening nevertheless. The couple had felt prepared and as ready as they could be for the public reaction but, as happens so often, their emotional and intellectual preparation did not entirely fit the actuality.

The initial flurry of press interest had been an irritation, increasing as the week progressed then dying out just as quickly as it had started. Of greater importance to Rebecca and Jean was how the people of Tarbert would react. They believed that the majority of villagers would initially recoil with surprise, shock even, then gradually become accustomed to the idea before returning to the usual relations. Rebecca had a view of the village entering a kind of extended seven-day wonder. They both had confidence in their friends, the same friends who had stayed by them during the tribulations of Jean's hospitalisation. Those good people had gone further in the direct provision of assistance than it was decent to expect. They were clearly special human beings and would not let something like a sex change interfere with friendship – they were above all that, were they not?

Truth was that Rebecca and Jean could not be sure how their announcement would affect people. A man adopting a feminine identity leading towards a sex change could raise all sorts of fundamental fears and prejudices lying dormant under the surface of the most liberal human beings, especially when it involved a close friend. Having dealt with the matter theoretically and intellectually, people are sometimes shaken by the nature and strength of their reaction when the issue enters their lives. Fear, disgust, confusion, worry and self-doubt all visit the most caring, capable people, regardless of their preparation.

Rebecca and Jean expected some people to have no comprehension, lacking the will even to attempt to understand. The couple anticipated a whole gamut of reactions to be evident and perhaps heaped on them and their family. Homophobia was rife in certain quarters and some would confuse the issue, finding it easier to view Rebecca (or Bob Pine as they would continue to call her) as a secret homosexual all his life and simply pursuing his sexual preference to the extreme. Others might see some freakish behaviour, being incapable of empathy with anyone other than their own identical image. Childhood is a time for cruelty and cruel the children were likely to be – with no intended malice – but cruel nevertheless. Certain adults were likely to view his plans, even his dressing, as a sin against God and, therefore, unforgivable. Other Christians would be much more charitable. Then there would be jokes, of course. Tarbert working-class humour had that wicked Glaswegian style about it and, in the way of that tradition, jokes would be made up by the local wags. There would be a Rebecca Series which would run until another target emerged. As with much of street culture, gags had a habit of enduring by becoming part of an extended repertoire to be dusted down and used when appropriate or, rather, most inappropriate.

On 11 October 1994, when Rebecca had first stepped out on to the streets of Tarbert, she really did not know how people would react.

It took a day or two for the first letter to arrive and then they kept coming addressed to 'Rebecca and Jean' or 'Dear Bob of the past and Rebecca of the future' and 'My dear friend and neighbour'. They contained such expressions as 'how privileged', 'how joyful' and 'thank you'. The letters came mainly from Tarbert though some from farther afield. They stated a unanimous support for Rebecca and Jean with declarations that 'nothing will change'. At worst they admitted 'shock' and a certain, initial awkwardness at the use of the name Rebecca for their friend, Bob. They asked for a little time to get used to it all – the villagers asked for forbearance – not for Rebecca but for themselves. Some friends did not send letters – they did not have to with their immediate and prompt appearance at the side of Rebecca and Jean Pine. They offered help, support or whatever was required. By asking, 'How can we help?' they had answered the question more than they could imagine.

The people of Tarbert had proved to be different in ways no one could have guessed except for the people of Tarbert. Rebecca and Jean Pine had friends.

Rebecca and Jean knew that not everyone was in the frame to accept the changes. There were those people struggling to make sense of it all who had gone quiet and those who quickly made a wrong sense of it all and refused to keep quiet. The troubles were far from over but with the declarations of support they had already received, Rebecca and Jean Pine felt strong enough to navigate any hazard.

As they drove to Inveraray Castle on the evening of 18 November, they were aware that they were about to partake in their first public engagement as Rebecca and Jean. They would meet people who had known them as Bob and Jean who would be meeting Rebecca for the first time. They would meet people who had never met them before and could react in different ways. They might also meet people who had read the press coverage and examined the photographs, bursting with sudden curiosity demonstrated through unintended rudeness. While Inveraray Castle was on familiar ground it was not the Pines' home turf. Rebecca and Jean were about to take their next risk.

The dance was to be held in The Saloon of the castle. Rebecca parked their car and with Jean entered through the main door. The splendour of the castle reached out and embraced them as it did with all who entered. It was impossible not to feel a sense of occasion as they walked through the Armoury Room with its ninety-five-foot-high ceiling, rows of Brown Bess muskets, Lochaber axes and Scottish broadswords, fanning up as high as the eye could see. Displayed in glass-topped cases were a collection of dirks and, in pride of place, Rob Roy MacGregor's sporran, belt and dirk sheath. The remnants of the life of another hero from another time.

As Rebecca and Jean entered The Saloon, they were not to be disappointed by the ambience of the room. Family portraits hung on the walls on enormous, intricately framed canvases and demonstrated the Duke's lineage and established the power of the clan over centuries. Through the windows in the far wall, a driveway led to sealed, heavy, metal gates and the original defence line. A heady mixture of safety, power and importance was the overall effect.

Rebecca and Jean were skilled and enthusiastic dancers. As the band started to play, their tapping toes and itchy feet dispelled the last vestiges of nervousness and off they went, dancing together as were other women in the company. An old failing of Scottish men in absenting themselves from dance through war, alcohol or mere reluctance served the Pines well. A proper Scottish country dance allows a short, breath-recovering interlude between each dance. Later that evening during such a break, flushed with the energy of their efforts, Rebecca and Jean stood and chatted under one of the long, wall-mounted symbols of Argyll's wealth. These were made of giltwood appliqués and in the fine, ornate work the letter 'A' could be discerned. Standing next to them, a man on his own joined in on their chat. The Pines had a conversational way with them that engaged the interest and invited participation of the casual eavesdropper. That same manner often resulted in first-time visitors to their shop pausing to explore some theme or whimsical comment and finding themselves still there half an hour later.

The man had never met the Pines before and his talk was of Argyll and Inveraray in particular. A visitor with an intelligent curiosity now applied to his plans for exploring the area, he found a ready source of information in his two new acquaintances. As the brief intermission was coming to an end, a friend of Jean's crossed the room and invited her to partner him in the next reel. Rebecca continued to speak with her companion, happy to describe Argyll and propose detours of interest. They spoke with each other over the strains of the band and through till the next pause in the programme. Jean had got caught up with some friends at the other side of The Saloon and

Rebecca was delighted to see her circulating and being made so obviously welcome by others.

As the fiddle and the accordion drew their breath, preparing for their next contribution, the man asked Rebecca to dance. Without hesitation she accepted and was walked out on to the floor by hand, ready for the reel. Skilled as she was in a multitude of dances, she mentally ran through the differences she would have to note – the differences between the male and the female steps. The music seemed sweeter, the movements more fluid and the timing just right. Sometimes it happened when a floor full of dancers and a five-piece band gel, getting everything just so, just as intended.

Mid-reel it struck home – she, a woman, had been asked to dance by a man. This stranger had accepted her for what she appeared to be, a woman. For the first time, a male was relating to her as a female and with all the social grace she had craved. Rebecca Pine had arrived.

A long time later, asked to recall how she felt during this first dance, Rebecca searched for the programme for that night in Inveraray Castle. Rummaging through a tin box of papers, she spoke about the dance. Unusually, she struggled to find words adequate to the task of describing her emotions. Finally extricating the dance programme from the bundle of papers, her cheeks glowed as she passed the printed card to the interested inquirer. Reading down the list, the music for that dance was *None So Pretty*. The question had been answered in full.

16 A Special Village,
a Special Wife

Sorrow and sighing shall flee away.
BOOK OF ISAIAH 35:10

Oban, Argyll. 1994.
Rebecca was not looking forward to this meeting. For what felt like an interminable age she had been attending appointments with psychiatrists, nurses and others. They were all very good and supportive but she wanted to get on with her journey and felt trapped in a state of limbo, an improvement on where she had been, but not yet at her destination.

The caring professions had been applying a range of devices to help her and to test her. She had decided unilaterally to live as a woman and was very much aware that she could be caught up in this half-way stage for two years or more. While keen to co-operate with the doctors, she found increasing difficulty in disguising her impatience and was nervous that this might be interpreted in other, negative ways. Rebecca would do as she was asked while quietly asserting her readiness to move on in her journey, ready for surgery.

Rebecca had never met the person before and had no idea if they had anything in common. The meeting simply represented another hurdle, another time-consuming act requiring a report to the psychiatrist and, presumably, his assessment. The meeting was with another applicant for a sex change operation, a man also living as a woman. Dr McCulloch expressed the hope that the two patients could offer each other some support and help through what was designed to be a stressful, demanding and lengthy process. They both might have to wait several years before achieving their ultimate goal and would need all the support they could muster. The idea was sound but was based

158

on the assumption that changing sex was sufficient grounds to forge a bond. Rebecca suspected that she and the other, we will call her Colleen, would become friends if they shared some interests in common – an overlapping view of the world, not of themselves. Rebecca had been given a photograph of Colleen and some basic background information. Colleen was much younger than Rebecca but that age gap would not present a difficulty in the two forming a friendship. The problem seemed to be that they lived different types of lives, had different interests and, Rebecca suspected, had quite disparate approaches to their sex change.

They met at the front in Oban, recognising each other immediately from the photographs. Both had been living and dressing as women for months previously and were therefore relaxed as they strolled along the busy Oban streets, stopping to window shop or to have a coffee. Colleen lived in a small island community and tended to be reclusive. She would escape on regular trips to Oban where she felt she could relax in a crowd.

The first difference between the two became evident: Colleen locked herself away at home most of the time, fearing hostility and being made a scapegoat by her community; Rebecca made a public announcement, appeared in the media, worked in the shop every day and pursued many social events; Colleen had separated from her wife; Rebecca and Jean were very much together. Rebecca Pine counted her blessings.

Throughout their few hours together, Colleen spoke of her fascination with new technology and her use of the Internet. From various sites she had collated information on hormones, drugs and treatments available to enhance femininity beyond the basic radical surgery. Colleen was keen to take advantage of all the help on offer and was enthusiastic to share the information with Rebecca. Over the months to come, the two would keep in touch by telephone and Rebecca would receive much more information about the various treatments the younger woman had unearthed. Rebecca wanted a nipped waist, large breasts, smoother skin and all the other shopping list of ideal attributes, but she did not want to pursue such a physique by the forced feeding of additional artificial substances. She was already taking the doses of oestrogen necessary to prepare the body for surgery and was happy at the early changes in her body.

Near the end of the afternoon, the two walked and chatted

around Oban town centre. Both acknowledged a need to go to the toilet and Colleen pointed the way, Rebecca following behind. Bypassing a range of available facilities, Colleen walked away from the shops beyond the periphery of the thoroughfare towards the Corran Halls, a large municipal building. Across from the Corran Halls there was a vast public toilet, much bigger than the usual scale of public convenience found in these parts. The toilet must have been constructed during better times, when tourism in Oban was high and the council purse stretched to meet the fundamental needs of visitors. Animated, Colleen led the way in through the Ladies entrance. Inside there was disappointment, in that the scale of the toilet allowed for no additional luxuries – just the usual closets, sinks, a long mirror and a great deal of space.

The visit to this cold, concrete barn was clearly a reason for excitement for Colleen. Rebecca realised that her new young acquaintance lived on a small island with few amenities. Watching Colleen fix her wig and make-up in the mirror, she thought of the young woman's reclusive, hideaway life. A life so lacking in joy and acceptance of her new-found femininity that walking through a doorway marked 'Ladies' in large, bold letters was enough to bring so much pleasure. Rebecca felt empathy with the young Colleen and knew that they were on the same side, but in very different regiments.

Driving home to Tarbert, Rebecca Pine considered herself to be a fortunate human being.

～

Tarbert, Argyll. 1994.
Some people in Tarbert were taking time to accept as ordinary the appearance of Rebecca Pine. To many of the working folk, a man had started dressing as a woman in public, no more than that. Worse, some still viewed Bob Pine as one of the upper class, someone who must have money, who spoke with posh tones, who had airs and graces. For some people, without these perceived advantages or distinctions, Bob Pine made a good target for ridicule and attack. He was not alone in this regard but had willingly provided a reason for the nonsense.

Jackie, Kirsty, their partners and children were ordinary, working people of Tarbert and had long been accepted as such. They circulated in the same jobs, attended the local primary school and socialised among the very people who were intent on making mischief about Rebecca Pine. Neighbours had long since ceased to cover up their discussions when Jackie walked past or to pretend that nothing had changed. Rebecca's emergence was a community issue and the daughters would have to cope with it somehow.

Jackie and Kirsty were strong individuals capable of coping with loose talk and much more. They had a resilience which comes to those who have had to move around and adjust to new towns, particularly as children. Their own children were a worry – such as when Nicole came home from school chanting a new skipping rhyme she had learned that day in the playground and the rhyme made fun of Rebecca, her grandfather. When Nicole learned the rhyme was about her grandfather she became very protective of her family, standing up for herself but running the risk of a renewed onslaught on herself. How does a parent deal with that?

The pressures would not go away either as long as they all lived in the village, which they all fully intended to do. So the children would face years of nasty teasing as would any other children coming along in the future. What about male children when they reached the formative, sensitive stage of puberty? Along with the nascent sexuality and adulthood might come innuendo, questioning their masculinity or their sexual preference and shaking an already uncertain time. Some adults in the village said things to the children, as if they somehow had the right to treat these children badly when they would not dare do the same to other children. As if the young ones did not have enough to cope with these days.

Jackie was worried about the day-to-day demands, simple things, usually, which had become so complex. Like what did they call Rebecca? Prior to the announcement it was 'Dad' or 'Grandad' but what now – 'Grandmother', 'Grandad Rebecca' or what? When Jackie thought of her stepfather she thought of him as Bob but in life he was to be called Rebecca. She could handle this enforced duality but what about the children? Her only hope was her belief that young ones had an innate sense of who the good, trustworthy people were and find Rebecca to be just so, while also finding an identity and an appropriate label. Trust the children to heal the wounds.

Time might also heal the tension and smooth the route for the children into adulthood. Sex changes were becoming more and more common and Jackie acknowledged that Rebecca and Jean had helped that process by their openness and honesty. Maybe in ten years, so many people would have a family or friendship connection to someone who had changed sex that it would cease to be a point of conversation, even for the bigots of life. Maybe, but Jackie could not be certain. Again it would be up to the children to take on the mantle of understanding that gender was a matter of personal choice. That correcting mistakes of birth was a right of all humans, a private business. So much was weighing on the children.

~

Tarbert, Argyll. 1995.
Walking, for Jean, had become a daily activity – not so much a habit or routine, really, but more a spiritual necessity. Through walking she found she could breathe and think and evaluate without interruption or irritation, something difficult for her to achieve in the company of others. It is not that she meant to be unreasonable but she had become trapped inside a consciousness she barely recognised to be her own at times. Before the accident she had always been clear-minded, certain and tolerant of others' failings. For years after her discharge from hospital she would catch herself breaking out in the most outrageous tantrums like an angry three-year-old child, stamping her feet and going red in the face with the exertion. All the while it was as if she was floating above her body, looking down on her performance and thinking she recognised herself behaving in a most uncharacteristic, unacceptable manner. Regardless of her ability to observe herself with disapproval, she remained powerless to halt the tirade.

She had been aware of her tendency to emotional outbursts for some time and needed to escape from that avenue, leading, as it did, nowhere useful. It was little consolation to Jean to know that her health and behaviour had improved immeasurably. She was not herself still. Now this business with Rebecca. How easily she had come to call her husband by that name. It felt strange but natural at the same time, as if she had known all along of Bob Pine's true identity. During her solitary walks, Jean had thought back to a night when she returned home early and found Robert among her things, her clothes. Or the time he had fallen from the loft – what was he doing up there and during the day when he ought to have been at work? Oh, she had been blind! She should have seen it earlier. Or, rather, she should have made Robert feel at ease so he felt able to tell her, his wife, sooner. With thoughts such as these, step after step, Jean reprimanded herself and searched for an answer without knowing the exact question.

At other times she wondered how she could cope. She had recently come to terms with the changes in herself and now this. She had chosen to live with and to marry someone who was charming, eloquent, artistic, caring and a handsome, fine figure of a man. She had married someone who had shared her interests, her passions and added some of his own which had infected her, converted her to other perspectives. Her handsome Bob had that effect on his Jean.

Sometimes on her walks she would despair that she had lost it all, everything which was precious to her. She believed she could cope with Rebecca in her current guise – her Bob dressing and living as a woman. Jean had even managed to laugh at the fuss and bother displayed by Rebecca in choosing a skirt to wear, searching for a clean pair of tights or messing with her wig to set it just so. That time, just after Rebecca's official emergence, when the sheep had chewed through the water pipes and there was a bit of heavy digging to do – what a laugh. Ashens Cottage was without water so action had to be taken, and fast. Digging had always been Bob's role especially since Jean's accident. Rebecca still met all of Bob's responsibilities without shirking any one of them, regardless how unladylike. So digging had to be done and Rebecca would fit the bill. Whereas another woman would change into clothes appropriate to the task (clearly trousers, wellington boots and heavy gloves) Rebecca had only too recently taken the right to wear frocks to concede now, even temporarily. Out in the rain went Rebecca, wearing skirt, blouse, lady's coat, head scarf and rubber boots. Okay for a piece of pottering in the garden, but not entirely suited to digging a trench in the heavy, oozing mud in the pouring rain. As she walked on, Jean laughed at the memory as only a friend and a lover can laugh.

Walking on up and around to Lady Ileene Road, Jean felt each step as she made the sharp ascent. She had spent time with her sister and her closest friend. She had stayed away for a period to get some clarity in her mind. She had spoken with Kirsty and Jackie, though Campbell did not want to say much.

Her son away in Stirling at the university worried her, so far away on his own and all this happening back home. He had cut himself off more and more and she knew through her sister that he was thinking of reverting to his natural father's name. Jean did not know if Rebecca's emergence had any influence on her son's deliberations or if he was trying to capture his own, true identity. It could even be that he preferred the name Todd to that of Pine. Jean knew it was so easy to believe that Rebecca had brought on all the changes around her, to blame her for everything which was so unfair. Jackie and Kirsty were not going to flee the village and encouraged Jean to stay close to them. Their first priority was their mother, worried that she was still physically frail and emotionally turbulent. They wanted their mother to be okay and to consider herself first and foremost.

For a time Jean had thought of leaving Rebecca and finding a house for herself. She had gone as far as applying for a council house and Kirsty had helped her, going along to meet with the council official. Kirsty had made sure that her mother's whole case was understood, not just the obvious changes in her marriage but also her personal needs and chronic ill health. Kirsty had not intended to be vindictive against Robert, as she still called her mother's husband, just protective of Jean. Along with so many others, Jean knew that both her daughters struggled to imagine themselves coping in similar circumstances. Thinking of their male partners deciding to become women was, for the girls, a theoretical exercise and they would leave the relationship forthwith – theoretically. They only wanted the best for Jean – in reality.

Reaching the top of Lady Ileene Road, Jean stopped to catch her breath. She found herself taking a rest at the war memorial, as so many before her and since. The levelled grass around the monument was trimmed short and benches were provided. Moving right to the peripheral fence, Jean looked out over Tarbert and watched the yellow lights of houses tweak on in a spattering of life, people preparing for the night that was approaching. At the far end of the harbour, the Crow's Nest loomed its dark hulk, stark in contrast against the blue-grey sky. Yellowed beams took life up there on the promontory houses, having been built on the massive rock which sheltered the village from southerly sea winds. She remembered her Robert on their first visit to the village, standing up there alone, quiet and deep with his thoughts and his dreams; emerging from his brief solitude, marching down the path, brisk and happy as if he had discovered some truth he wished to share with the world; the five of them congregating by the loch and celebrating a shared wish to move to this place. In that moment, the talk was of the practical affairs of selling up, dates, schools and jobs but there was something else, something profound and unspoken between her and her man. With a look and a smile they both knew they had found their place, their future together and each other.

Jean stood and watched the light change from day to night over Tarbert and far out over the loch. The grey-blue moved to a hue of navy blue, not bleak or soulless but a colour, deep and warm. Night – the time for rest, warmth and dreams. Jean had shared her dreams with Robert and her dreams had not changed. Her Robert had become Rebecca and what had changed? Rebecca was the same charming, eloquent, artistic, caring person Robert had been. The same person who could nurse her through her agonies for years, because of love and no thought of obligation. The same person who had carried a hidden ache, almost forever, and now was free of it for the first time. Rebecca was her Robert who needed Jean's care, now as never before.

Moving away from the view over the sleep-walking village, Jean started off towards home and the person who shared her dreams. Musing on the price people paid for love, Jean felt light-hearted and happy for the first time in an age. Jean Pine thought of herself as a very fortunate woman. She had decided to stay with her Rebecca.

17 From Chrysalis
to Butterfly

In sunlight or in shade at every phase
From chrysalis to butterfly they cared,
Their strength, their love, in fond remembrance stays
This family who my emergence shared.
REBECCA PINE IN 'FROM CHRYSALIS TO BUTTERFLY'

The Surgery, Tarbert, Argyll. 1996.
Dr McCulloch had been inspirational and friendly, as well as a psychiatrist. Rebecca's meetings with him were almost like popping in to visit an old chum; almost, but not quite. The psychiatrist conveyed the impression of someone who had a mixed and varied life, with his work being one component only. His approach to his work, with Rebecca at least, felt as if he was genuinely interested in her situation and would have been willing to help whether or not he was being paid. In short, Rebecca trusted Dr McCulloch.

One day he had to discuss with her some concerns which, for a change, had little to do with her, how she was living, feeling or relating to others. The psychiatrist wanted to talk of administration. The start of the conversation felt like an irrelevance to Rebecca – pleasant enough, but nothing to do with her situation. A reorganisation of administration was to take place and was having an impact on the overall management of health services to Argyll and Bute. This was part of the government's policy in terms of the devolution of responsibility to business units with the aim of increasing efficiency. Generally the experience of the medical profession had been that the sought-after efficiency was a paper exercise and, in truth, fewer services were being delivered with more money being spent on the salaries of those employed to run the

Health Trusts. If not exactly jaundiced, most doctors were certainly sceptical of the benefits of the new Trusts.

Sex-change surgery was an expensive procedure. Many applicants were forced to pay for the operation privately. Rebecca had made it plain that she wanted the National Health Service to meet the costs in her instance. Dr McCulloch considered Rebecca Pine to be a worthwhile case and supported her application for NHS resources. Here was the nub of the conversation: a change of administration meant different people; different people in positions of authority and holding budgets; a smaller financial kitty, less likely to afford one-off expensive operations; a setting-up time when key personnel would be fully engaged in establishing the organisation, possibly delaying decisions on non-urgent treatment. Sex changes were not usually deemed to be urgent or life threatening, though sadly this point of view proved to be spurious as some patients took their own lives, torn and weary from years of waiting.

The psychiatrist was convinced that Rebecca was ready for surgery. Rebecca knew she had been ready for a change of sex all her life. The bureaucratic nightmare and fiscal confusion of government policies had been most unwelcome in many places but here brought forth a gift to Rebecca Pine. The psychiatrist had accelerated the application and a date had been set for the radical surgery. Rebecca was to be admitted to Ashdown Hospital, West Sussex, towards the end of July, 1996. All being well, the operation was likely to take place on 31 July. Less than two years after that first confession, after Jean's careless exhortation about going 'the whole hog', Rebecca Pine would be truly and fully released into the world.

Walking back to the shop from the surgery, Rebecca thought of all the information on sex changes she had collected over the years. She had gleaned a great deal of facts among the rubble of the fiction. Facts such as the difficulty in convincing British doctors of your resolve, the likelihood that some, if not all, of the costs would have to be self-funded, like the waiting period going on for years and years. The speed of delivery and quality of service seemed to be influenced by which part of the country you lived in, with rural areas having a poor track record. Here she was in one of the remotest parts of Britain being helped to take her journey to its conclusion and in record time. 'Less than two years, all in all. I waited a lifetime but in the end it was only two years,' she thought, as she strolled in the sun in her favourite part of the world.

Rebecca Pine knew that she had been a lucky man and was soon to be a lucky woman.

~

Ashdown Hospital, Hayward's Heath, Sussex, England. 1996. Rebecca had driven down on her own the day before. She did not need to calculate the miles or pay much attention to the route, her knowledge of the country and experience of driving long distances standing her in good stead. Hayward's Heath was somewhere on the outskirts of London on the Brighton side and finding the hospital would be the only complication. Tarbert to Brighton was a considerable distance, four hundred miles or something like that she thought, but it never crossed her mind to travel in any mode of transport other than by car. Anyway, there were few other means of getting to Glasgow, two hours away, where she would have to go to catch a train or a flight. As with many of the Argyll people, she simply got in the car, pointed it in the right direction and left.

Travelling was such a routine chore it was usually boring, but not this journey. As Rebecca drove her way down the twisting, winding roads to Glasgow and beyond, on the first of a series of mind-numbing motorways, she would catch herself smiling for no particular reason other than the purpose of the journey itself. Watching Rebecca as she drove smiling to herself, being courteous to other drivers, all the while listening to the rise and fall of orchestral music, one might imagine that she was off on holiday or on her way to meet a long-lost friend.

Preparation for the surgery had been detailed but the intricacies were something she was not that interested in, unlike Colleen who was fast becoming a repository for specialist and detailed information. Rebecca was much more interested in the freedom and ease which the surgery would bring. She co-operated fully with all the medical requirements which lately had mainly consisted of an increase in her dosage of oestrogen. She looked this hormone up in a health encyclopaedia and had noted the contents with a grin when she read, 'In men, oestrogens have no known specific function.'

The hormone was to replace her lack of ovaries, something the best surgeon could not create, yet. Rebecca Pine would be a sixty-five-year-old woman and had no need of functioning ovaries. She had need of smoother skin, a higher voice, breasts and a waist. These aspects of her body and presentation appeared to have developed since she started living as a woman and taking the oestrogen. Rebecca found it difficult to attribute all her changes to the hormone or to the freedom of expression her chosen lifestyle had allowed. She felt more feminine than ever before and seemed to become more woman than man, week by week. Drugs or socialisation, nurture or nature, she did not know. Neither did she know if her gender confusion had been caused by an accident of birth or by social experiences and influences as a child. She did not know nor did she much care. Rebecca knew how she felt and was soon to feel whole.

Finding the hospital with some difficulty, Rebecca drove round the building, finding a parking space at the rear. The hospital was a modern, hospitable-looking place and inside it felt more like a hotel than the grey, disinfectant-reeking places of her childhood. Ashdown was a private hospital and one of the few centres of excellence for sex-change operations in Britain. Rebecca was not entirely sure how the arrangements worked but assumed that the National Health Service found it less expensive to buy in these services than to provide them. It was also curious that at that time this West Sussex hospital was the place Scottish applicants were sent for sex-change treatment. She did not much care about the business strategy, focusing entirely on her conviction that she was about to receive the best treatment available.

Mr Michael Royle was the surgeon – one of the foremost specialists in his field. Meeting with Rebecca the day before the scheduled surgery, the doctor was required to assess that his patient understood what was to happen and wished to proceed. This was a lengthy, intricate operation, extreme enough to be dangerous and likely to result in a painful recovery period. It was expected that the most committed patient would be nervous, anxious and fearful. All the patients wished to be female but that did not dispel their human instinct to avoid pain and choose life.

Rebecca smiled in response to the surgeon's questions; he commented that he had rarely encountered a more relaxed, content individual in any context, never mind in a pre-operative hospital ward. Mr Royle wasted little time with Rebecca and, grasping her hand, said that he looked forward to meeting with her the next day in theatre. As the surgeon moved out of Rebecca's single room, she thought to herself that the surgeon was not looking forward to the next day nearly as much as she was.

~

Operating Theatre, Ashdown Hospital. 31 July 1996.
Rebecca accepted the pre-med drugs with good grace, though they were really not necessary. Draped in the usual ridiculous operating gown and with her pubic hair shaved, she awaited the trolley and the ride to the operating theatre with a smile. The operation lasted several hours, the task being one of rebuilding rather than removal. The surgeon seemed to think of the surgery in the same way as his patient – as giving rather than taking away.

Rebecca suspected that some of the occasional hostility she had met from young, posturing, macho males had something to do with their own fear. Many a man while watching slap-stick comedy, fully aware it is all acting and fiction, will wince when a hapless character gets kneed in the testicles. Most of the males in the audience will grimace, groan and involuntarily reach between their legs for self-protection. If the symbolism of *The Benny Hill Show* or a Brian Rix farce is so strong, what is the impact of your neighbour seeking to have his genitals removed?

The textbook would describe the operation quite simply: the erectile tissue of the penis is removed; the urethra is repositioned to allow future urination; the skin of the penis is inverted into the body, creating a vaginal lining within the perineum; the testicles are removed; the skin of the scrotum is then formed into a labium. Of course, the bodily parts belong to someone and are as intimate and warm to the patient as the scalpel is objective and cold to the surgeon. Thus, that day, the old Robert Pine was transformed in textbook fashion.

The surgeon can go far in making a vagina which looks and functions like a vagina, depending on how much material he has to work with and how far the patient wants him to proceed. The old Robert Pine's penis and scrotum were transformed into fully functioning female genitals with the exception of the ability to ovulate or procreate. Aged sixty-five years, the lack of maternal capacity was not an issue and besides, that was not the point, not the point at all. Nothing was lost that day – a woman was found.

~

Ashdown Hospital, Hayward's Heath. 1 August 1996.

The half-waking state in emerging from a general anaesthetic had the usual feel of being exhausted and unwell, asleep but not rested. In such a state people are prone to differing conclusions dependent on their state of mind or the purpose of the treatment. They lie on their recovery beds rejoicing in their survival or praying for the success of the blade. They lie on their beds struggling to breathe through congested and choking nasal canals and wish themselves somewhere else. They despair at the arid desert of their mouths and plead in croaking voice for water, a little water, and grown adults want to cry when the kindly but firm nurse refuses. Mostly they feel sorry for themselves and wish it all over and done with.

Through the haze of the drugs, Rebecca began to celebrate. Whatever the demands and discomfort she felt, they were a little price to pay and would quickly shift. Soon she would feel herself and be her new self, a new woman.

Considerable pain is expected in the aftermath of a sex change operation. The reorganisation of the old male genitalia requires considerable cutting, stretching and trimming. The creation of the new female genitalia requires a great deal of healing and knitting together of tissue. Pain is inevitable and each patient is counselled that the agony is part of the creation of their new self, a good sign meaning that the operation has worked and their female physique is taking final form. Rebecca waited for the pain in stoic manner. She waited and waited over those first few days, confined to bed and engrossed in the fragile state of her body. She was still waiting when four days after the operation she was allowed out of bed for the first time and assisted in having a bath.

Each step had to be taken with great care to avoid any damage to her newly constructed area. The walk to the bathroom was not far but seemed to take an age, not just because of the trepidation of aggravating the wounds but in anticipation of recovery. That first trip out of bed was the most significant indication that Rebecca was becoming stronger and soon might be fit enough for the outside world.

Helped into the bath by a nurse, Rebecca sat alone and naked for the first time since her operation. Fresh wounds are never a welcome or pretty sight, revealing the ravages of the surgeon's knife in slicing the skin and folding the flesh. Patients are often warned of the possibility of distress on first viewing the healing scars, blood-encrusted and iodine-stained. If this applies to a foot, arm or leg then what is the impact of viewing your genitals all cut and swollen? If you have encountered and held your penis several times a day; if, when you look at yourself naked in the mirror, that dangling maleness is part of you; if you have treated your testicles with care, avoiding damage in a ruck and folding them carefully in your trousers; and if all that and more has been part of you every day for almost sixty-six years, what do you think and feel as you look down to see them gone?

Rebecca sat in the bath and looked down. Where others would see a disfigurement or mutilation she saw her real self. Her pudenda were visible and fully formed with mons venus and protruding vaginal lips. Still hairless from the necessary indignity of the pubic shave, she recalled models in life art classes in the 1950s where even in art, the display of bodily hair was frowned upon. The models, usually women, would stand stark naked for hours before a group of young adults, examining each curve and crevice of nakedness in front of them, sometimes moving close to check an angle, see the texture. Rebecca could not recall if the models removed their pubic hair through some code of public decency, for aesthetic enhancement or artistic trend. It did not matter to her that day for what she recalled was the young man, Robert, one of the voyeuristic artists holding that each and every one of those exposed women were, quite simply, lovely.

Looking down at her genitalia, Rebecca did not see a healing wound or traumatised flesh but her own, beautiful self. Rebecca Pine felt no pain that day or ever from her change of sex.

~

Ashdown Hospital, Hayward's Heath. 5 August 1996.
The time after that first, creative surgery was a time of celebration for Rebecca Pine. She was still required to walk and move with care, but she met each day with growing strength, knowing it drew her closer to the outside world and a return to her life. Since that first conversation with Jean less than two years ago, Rebecca found herself eager to proceed and increasingly intolerant of delay or purposeless prevarication. Normally full of patience, she had waited for sixty-five years and did not wish to wait a minute longer than necessary. She gave some thought to others finding themselves in her position with the need to change sex and suspected that once admitted, they all wanted to escape to their real selves immediately – much

like being caught in a trap where the knowledge itself of entrapment creates the desperation for release.

Rebecca's stay in Ashdown was as pleasant as a hospital stay could be and the essential care and attention received helped her accept the necessary delay in pursuing her life. In truth, Rebecca Pine would walk through fire and more to achieve the femininity of her spirit. Perhaps the strength of Rebecca's determination aided her recovery, for she made rapid progress. The consultant had advised that she was well enough to go home and a date had been agreed for the following week. She would meet with Mr Royle on one final occasion on her last day but he had already prepared her for some of the required routine which would become part of her daily existence as well as other options she might wish to consider: options such as prosthetics or breast implants, not paid for by the NHS since reckoned not to be essential. Liposuction, hair weaves and a variety of drug treatments enhancing different aspects of the feminine physique could be pursued to create the kind of body she wished or as close a proximity as possible.

The creation of female genitalia is not a permanent act, with the vaginal lips having a tendency to knit together and close. Rebecca was advised that she would be required to ensure that her vaginal opening was stimulated and entered every day without fail or risk the inevitable. There were two major and obvious ways to achieve this: penetrative sex; or artificial dilation. A nurse would come by later to explain further. Rebecca could not wait for the nurse's story.

She breezed into Rebecca's room, holding aloft a long, narrow box much as harmonicas are stored in, just thicker.

'Look what I've brought for you!' was the nurse's announcement, clearly displaying that she enjoyed this part of her work. Closing the door behind her, the nurse laid the box gently in front of Rebecca, 'It's your sex life!'

The nurse explained again to Rebecca the absolute necessity of ensuring that her vagina was opened on a daily basis and quickly ran through the terrible consequences if she failed in this. The medic explained that some transsexual women choose to sleep with a man or men on a regular basis and made it plain that she considered them lucky, having a need for sexual intercourse as prescribed on medical grounds. The absolute cure for brewer's droop, long absences on the golf course or any other version of 'Not tonight, Josephine'. It was further explained that some heterosexual transsexuals chose to sleep around, ensuring a ready supply of fresh and willing men; the nurse's disapproving 'tsk tsk' heavy with irony.

Of course, the nurse went on to describe certain situations where men get in the way and home entertainment was useful and often better. With a flourish she lifted the lid of the box and lovingly removed the contents – a device of penis shape and size. The National Health Service had afforded a dildo, for that was how the object would be described in a sex show or at an Anne Summers party. Rebecca's nurse would have been a great hit at the direct selling and illustration of sex toys; she was an expert in the description and illustration of lubrication, insertion and frequency. On the last point she was most emphatic: 'Daily – at least. More often if you wish.' A further explanation was offered that this was a most convenient toy which travelled well. It could be used by oneself in the privacy of your home, a hotel room or anywhere with a bed. Some transsexual women are homosexual and encourage their lesbian partners in the use of the 'joystick'. Again the nurse hinted with a sigh that she considered such recipients fortunate indeed.

Performance over, the nurse left the room with a final earthy comment, leaving Rebecca convinced that there was a woman who had no need of a doctor's prescription to meet her own sexual needs. She had left Rebecca feeling grateful for her sense of humour and enthusiasm. What could have been a cold, clinical lecture was turned by that nurse into a warm, human exchange. She had treated Rebecca as a sexual equal and a trustworthy recipient of personal and sexual confidences.

Rebecca Pine was not about to become promiscuous as a heterosexual or homosexual. She had been talking dirty – woman to woman – for the first time in her life and she was grateful to that nurse.

~

Ashdown Hospital, Hayward's Heath. 9 August 1996.
The last meeting with Mr Royle was almost emotive for Rebecca. She was aware that the consultant had final authority on her preparedness for discharge from hospital and may well conclude that she should stay for a few days more. The prospect did not cross her mind more than fleetingly. The emotion came

from her confidence that in an hour she would be heading off towards home, Jean and a new life.

Rebecca was checked out physically and was found to be as well as expected a couple of weeks after undergoing major surgery. The consultant made various short enquiries on her well-being and appeared to be satisfied with her responses. Mr Royle confirmed that she could leave that day then gave her advice and instructions on taking care of herself. He reminded Rebecca that she had spent many hours on the operating table and lost large amounts of blood. These factors aligned with her recent confinement to a hospital room would result in her being weaker than she might expect. The doctor also reminded his patient that her genitalia were still forming and binding, consisting still of a considerable amount of torn tissue and skin. It was paramount that she did nothing to jeopardise the healing process, so no lifting, work or driving for at least a month. Rebecca nodded in agreement with everything the doctor said. Wishing her the best of luck and receiving sincere gratitude in return, the doctor left Rebecca's room, turning his attention to the next person on his list.

Already packed, Rebecca said her farewells and thanks to nursing staff, while leaving other patients with her sincere good wishes for the future. Leaving by the main door of the hospital she walked round the building to where she had left her car parked weeks before. Looking up at the hospital she scanned the building and checked – and was almost sure she could not be seen from the ward she had just left. Knowing that it was too late now for hesitation, she sat gingerly in the driver's seat and drove away. Two minutes out of the hospital and she was already breaking the rules. Rebecca Pine had changed, but not that much.

18 A Return Journey

Surprised by joy – impatient as the Wind
I turned to share the transport – Oh! With whom
But Thee, deep buried in the silent tomb.
WILLIAM WORDSWORTH IN 'SURPRISED BY JOY'

Newman wondered why her walks seemed to take place as night fell. She did not plan her strolls that way, in fact she never planned to go for a walk, believing exercise to be a waste of time. She would find herself in the village for a meal or sitting in the cottage alone and drunk and suddenly need the space, the cold and the movement. Newman did not walk anywhere else but Tarbert. She did not walk for the good of her body but for the good of her mind.

She liked it there up by Tarbert Castle where she had met her sole Argyll friend. Now long gone with his family, she had received a letter from his wife, explaining that he was not well. Within months of moving to Stornoway he had begun to fret of social chaos, anarchy, exploitation, drugs and despair. All his bogeymen visited him at the same time and out there where his family had no connection, no support, no reliable base. He had started to drink heavily and privately, sitting in a darkened room, morose and angry. His wife despaired but became fearful of the gentle, caring husband she had known as he answered her concerns for his welfare with raging tempers and eventually violence.

Newman's friend had been admitted to a psychiatric hospital away from the family home where he had come to live alone, his wife taking the children and fleeing for safety back to the mainland, to the city of their origins. The psychiatrist had written to her stating that her husband was clinically depressed and suicidal. The doctor appealed for her help, expressing pessimism in his ability to help his patient, all drug therapy being ruined by chronic alcohol dependence.

The wife was torn apart, wanting to help but not willing for her children to return to the nightmare of life with their father. Her usually sociable and outgoing husband had made no friends in the Western Isles, his last real connection being with Newman. The woman pleaded with Newman to visit her husband, just one visit to see if contact from the recent past would help. Her husband used to rant in his alcoholic stupor, going on and on about how people let him down and that Newman's splendid isolation had been the right way after all. On and on and on – openness and honesty being just a fool's game allowing people to use you then walk away when you needed them. Newman had it right – the only real friend he ever had . . .

Newman cursed the woman's letter and her own stupidity for taking this turn up towards Tarbert Castle where she had first met her friend. She would not go to Stornoway, of course, though she might write a letter. She did not feel good about denying help but really did not think it was any of her business. She was angry with the wife for trying to drag her into this affair and gave a bitter laugh at the postscript to her letter, the bit about the divorce and thinking of getting married again. If the wife was running away, Newman should not feel bad about her own reluctance to help. Trouble was, she had met the fellow up here by the castle and every step was making her feel heavy in spirit, almost sad. 'Honesty and openness,' she thought. 'No wonder you were ranting. Absolutely right in your madness. Never did anybody any good. Brings nothing but trouble.' Newman was fast convincing herself that her friend was not ill at all. He had merely come to understand a truth and could not cope with a revelation which contradicted and shattered the basis of his life thus far.

Standing on a raised lip affording a view down the loch in the direction of Lochgilphead and beyond, Newman felt her usual creeping comfort, watching the low-hung fog, wheezing and alive, crawling over and enshrouding all in its path. Bad weather here was surely glorious. The street lights and cottage roofs down below still penetrated the dense, wet blanket and she recognised the slates of Springside Cottage. She could identify that house from any angle in any light or no light, so long and hard had she stared at its structure wishing grief upon the inhabitants. No point in staring now; the Pines had truly fled, nesting outside the village in that isolated, roadside house, Ashens Cottage. Newman's chance to wish ill upon the Pines was reduced to fleeting moments as she drove in and out of Tarbert, speeding past in her car. She still thought of her old acquaintance as Bob Pine and when using the name Rebecca, spat it out with vehemence and envy.

Openness and honesty. Newman thought that liberal-minded observers would attribute those strengths to that man who had kept himself a secret for so many years. Newman believed that Bob Pine had played around with people for so long, living his life the way he wanted, paying the lowest price and taking the easiest route. Only when he could hide no longer and was certain of the support of his wife and these Tarbert people did he come out and be truthful. Typical of Bob Pine: all show and drama, going the whole way, smiling all the while.

Newman savoured a memory, familiar ground to her drunken Tarbert staggers, yet tasty still. Army days and a play in Newquay, a great success for the entertainment-starved populace; a jape for most of the soldiers, allowing time away from camp, a drink and the chance to meet others; Bob Pine taking it so seriously in that easy-going but intense manner of his, infuriating; the laugh at Pine all full of booze and spewing over that lady officer, twice. Newman had watched Bob Pine then, interested and curious, believing there was more to the soldier. He was surprised when Bob did not turn up at any of the known pubs or party houses. The scene was safe enough, especially among the Army boys with everyone depending on each other to keep their secret.

Newman thought that Bob Pine was more feminine than any of the other boys. The way he walked, held his hand when speaking and his smile. Some of the guys were hard nuts, thugs really, but they all fancied Pine. Mind you, so did most of the women they met in the bars. Newman had come to the view that Bob Pine was just scared until that day he followed him to the refuge dump and watched him surreptitiously stick a bundle deep into a bin. Waiting till the depositor had marched off, Newman had dug through the rubbish till he found the parcel, covered in peelings and miscellaneous goo.

The day Newman found the disposed-of women's clothing was the day he started to hate Bob Pine. Sergeant Bob Pine was obviously a lot like Newman and the others, just too much of a snob, sticking to his own kind or the officers or whatever. But

Newman knew he had the proof that Bob Pine was just like him.

The years after National Service had been hard for Newman. No job, no money, no prospects and no place to go. Until his special friend turned up in his life and showed him what he could be if he wanted. When his friend disappeared without word or farewell, Newman started to rebuild himself. He swore there would be no more darkened toilets: he moved across the city, reappearing with a different name, different clothes, different identity. His friend had taught him much but not how to speak, how to walk in heels, to sit down with his knees together. So many things to learn, so few friends, so many beatings. Yet Newman had survived and made his way and no one challenged him anymore about being a man in woman's clothes. No drugs, no help, no snip, snip operation – just him as her, as Newman.

Newman would not forget Bob Pine. He was just a man the same as him, he thought, no difference really. They were all playing a part and Newman could not explain it any other way. Looking down on Springside, the symbol and focus of so much anger, Newman spat, 'Rebecca Pine, you make me angry for taking so long and going so far.'

19 Freedom is . . .

that I should be
that person that I always was
but have not always been.
REBECCA PINE IN 'MY FREEDOM'

Kiltie's Shop, Tarbert, Argyll. 1998.
The shop seemed somehow crowded with people, not hard given its size, but unusually sustained for long periods. All morning there had been a stream of customers, a mixture of local people, tourists and those passing through on their way east or west. In the background the radio played as usual, classical music quietly humming and strumming and soothing away the worries. Jean and Rebecca had been required to serve most of the time with little opportunity for checking stock or making out order sheets. Two cups of tea, barely sipped, sat on the counter weeping for replenishment.

People could now choose where to buy their newspapers from several shops in Tarbert. Four years earlier, an unspoken agreement whereby Kiltie's sold the Sundays and the others specialised in the dailies had somehow fallen apart for reasons which remained unclear. First one then the other of the established newsagents started to open on Sundays to be augmented by a fourth when the Post Office shop entered the market. The result was four small shops opening at dawn each day, all selling all the newspapers and working harder and harder for smaller and smaller returns. While purchasers came from much farther afield than Tarbert, the market remained too small to support so many shops. The customers were spoiled for choice and if choosing on convenience, were unlikely to walk the extra yards to Kiltie's. But the shop prospered because many of the public chose on loyalty or because they enjoyed the chat and the feeling of welcome.

On busy days like that morning, Rebecca and Jean marvelled at their ability to go on. The night before they had returned home late from a Scottish Opera performance in Glasgow. Empowered and invigorated as ever by the depth of the music, they were nevertheless worried a little as they neared home. A landslide had recently brought a mountain of rock down, closing the main road to Tarbert and, while reopened two days before, there was little guarantee of this being sustained. A landslide of similar proportions had closed the road at the same spot earlier in the year and had been mended after a long period of uncertainty and inconvenience. The Council advised of their thorough efforts to ensure a permanent repair only for a repeat performance.

The road was open and the two women sallied home, late but not as late as they feared. The mid-Argyll area was developing a habit of geological phenomena with landslides and earthquakes. Global warming was predicted to raise the sea level and wild loons were suggesting that the peninsula of Kintyre would be cut off at the isthmus, at Tarbert, and become the island some already considered it to be. Some would say this was also a magical place where nothing was as it seemed nor would stay as expected. Spring full moons hanging over the village like enormous planets coming to rest gently on the earth enhanced this view. So, too, did the standing stones and ancient grounds, here found casually in a copse of trees, often unfenced, unmarked and left to devices which survived centuries; and sightings of roaming black pumas, spotted at night on the edge of forests, staring back through diamond-lit eyes before turning and slinking off into the mess of trees. Witches, sorcery and moon worship were all rumoured to flourish still and, when asked, wry locals would not admit the charge, while ensuring they would not deny it.

The place was magical, of course, in the way all special places embrace the people and keep them there for ever, making do in the only place they can feel whole. Thus Rebecca and Jean Pine drove round trips of two hundred miles several times a month to watch a play or hear a concert but always came back, returning home to the only place they could live and be their entire selves.

~

Standing at the front of the queue, four other customers waiting patiently behind, was a local man in the habit of stopping for a chat about the weather, the wildlife and a certain quiz on an afternoon radio programme. Most days Rebecca and Jean would happily talk, pleased to share their time and delight in his conversation. The man was quite oblivious to the shuffling feet and nervous coughs. When he went into Kiltie's he always stopped for a blether, so blether he would; no ill intended, it was just what he did – when he went into Kiltie's.

~

The queue moved down and the shop now cleared, Rebecca proposed a fresh brew of tea and Jean made it, their old roles preserved, unchanging. Sipping the tea as they stood behind the counter and chatting about the concert of the night before, aspects returned to haunt them sweetly. Two women entered the shop, tourists from Maryland in America. A typical exchange of comments ensued with the visitors lauding the scenic beauty of the area and the quaint ache of Tarbert. Rebecca and Jean were conversationalists – unusual in these parts since, unlike most, they were not content only to give out information but also sought it, being interested in all people and their habitats. The discussion developed further and longer than most, reaching the stage of exchanging names and gifts. From Rebecca, a book of her *Tarbert Poems*; from the American ladies, photographs of their home town.

In twenty minutes the four women had clicked and were almost reluctant to part. Expressing how much she had enjoyed their brief meeting, one of the American women wondered out loud about the relationship between Rebecca and Jean: 'Are you sisters?' she offered, going on some premise regarding the two women having the same surname. Receiving no immediate response she assumed she was wrong so she tried, 'Sisters-in-law?'. Still no response, so quickly and finally, 'Cousins?' Lost for a ready-made answer and being sure these kindly people did not wish to hear the full unexpurgated version, Rebecca smiled and replied, 'Yes, that will do . . .'

~

As the man entered the shop, Jean spotted him first and smiled at Rebecca who rolled her eyes, grimaced and wished him a good morning heartily, cheerily. The two women were used to his visits to the shop, two, maybe three times each week. Aged somewhere in his seventies, the silver-haired man always dressed as if he had stepped off his ocean-going yacht, resplendent in captain's hat, dark blazer and light-coloured slacks. He had moved to Kintyre many miles from the village a few months earlier. Stopping at Kiltie's periodically to buy his cigarettes and newspapers was understandable, if he happened to be passing through. Travelling here especially to buy a mere twenty pack of Benson and Hedges and sometimes a bar of chocolate was taking customer allegiance too far.

His routine and purpose were well established and served to amuse rather than irritate Rebecca and Jean. He had fallen for Rebecca and in his gentle, manly way was endeavouring to work his way into her favour. None too subtle in his approach, he was harmless and complimentary. Both women had their admirers and would-be suitors as happens when you serve the public. A sitting target, customers' frequent visits allow an opportunity to appraise, to become fond of and ultimately fall for the object of their attention. Rebecca and Jean were objects of desire for certain men.

⌒

The hours passed and Rebecca was due to take care of business in the village. For two individuals of creative and liberal style, both Jean and Rebecca were required to fulfil certain routine obligations to keep the shop organised. Those who knew the women believed such mundane obligation must grate against their spirit but they appeared to bear the load with tolerance as a small price for their lifestyle and relative freedom from heavier loads. At the first possible opportunity that day, Rebecca left the shop and set off on her business.

Rebecca and Jean had an unspoken arrangement that such separations would be explained and not of undue duration. Jean still became anxious when unsupported over prolonged periods, though her health had improved beyond all expectations and predictions. The commitment to each other was no overbearing burden and easy to manage. Most of what they did they did together by choices made before the accident. Jean knew that

Rebecca would be gone for no more than half an hour and could cope with much longer separations when necessary.

Rebecca stepped out into the sudden, sharp sunlight, drawing her coat around her body, shielding herself from the cold, crisp air and walked purposefully towards the bank. No sooner had Rebecca left the shop than Jean's attention was attracted by two young female customers. Jean put aside her book, wondering how many times in all had she started that particular paragraph, lifted her head and was ready, once again, to serve.

A little later than she planned, Rebecca returned to Kiltie's prepared to recount to Jean the confusion she had suffered in some transaction or another. Now, when leaving Jean on her own, Rebecca was always a little anxious for her partner though understood this to be unnecessary, neurotic almost. She thought that she would never fully recover from seeing her Jean cut, broken and apparently lifeless. During all that first year, when the doctors were not sure if Jean would live and if she survived what the quality of her life might be, Rebecca had not been as pessimistic, had never given up hope, but never stopped worrying. She wondered if this anxiety was just a symptom of love and one of the prices to be paid. With an aftertaste of unease, Rebecca breezed into their small emporium and was relieved to find Jean sitting behind the counter engrossed in reading one of her current books.

Happy to let her partner rest and read and feeling almost content at the lull of customers, for the moment, Rebecca took off her coat, rubbing her hands together and chattered on inanely about how cold it was in spite of the blue sky – all in the manner which means 'I expect no reply'. Some minutes later Jean sat up with a start, snapped her book shut and began to tell a story, excited, almost enthralled. It sometimes happened that Jean's short-term memory lapses played delay-device tricks with the potential for humour in their impact as she answered a question, precisely and accurately, but asked two sentences before. Something similar had happened that day and this is the thrust of the tale Jean intended to tell Rebecca the minute she walked through the doorway:

The two female callers had not been customers but one had met Rebecca and decided to look her up as she passed through Tarbert. The red-haired young woman, as Jean recalled, spoke in couched, careful terms to begin with, as if feeling the way to ascertain who she was addressing. Realising that Jean was Rebecca's partner, the information flowed from the red-head in a rapid flourish. Jean was having to work hard to keep up with the rate and order of her speech and was catching words and phrases here and there such as 'Internet', 'Irish ferry', 'breast implants', 'lesbian' and 'lover'.

Jean saw a striking young woman, clear and confident as well as obviously happy. She made no effort to conceal her affection for her female companion. As the time dragged on and it was certain that Rebecca had been delayed, Jean began to probe with questions in a gentle inquisitorial style, learned long ago as a school teacher. The woman had had a sex-change operation and had hidden herself away for years. She spent all her money on enhancing her female body and all her time communicating with the outside world through the medium of her computer. She had joined a site specialising on personal introductions and, declaring herself to be a transgendered female, sought lesbian lovers with considerable success. The woman with her was her latest date and they had just spent the week together in Argyll. Colleen had been driving her new-found lover to Campbeltown, to catch her return ferry home to Ireland, when she decided to look in on Rebecca.

Colleen planned to move away from Argyll to a city where she could be among people, perhaps work for an employer and be part of an active and accessible lesbian scene. She had discovered herself and was keen to let Rebecca know that they were on the same side still and she thought of her acquaintance now and then. Before she could see Rebecca she had had to leave and drive her friend to the ferry. A recluse no more, Colleen was alive in the world and loving women as a woman.

~

By mid-afternoon, the rate of customers had slowed to an almost negligible trickle. As was their habit during the quiet season, Jean and Rebecca agreed to shut up the shop and head home. They busied themselves in a familiar series of duties, each with her specialism, each with her part to play. Rebecca had often thought that as someone who had made a dreadful soldier, she was borrowing from the Army's approach now, dealing with the boring necessities of life by rote. Such an allocation of tasks simply meant that the place was shut up quickly and everything was done.

Carrying the small bundle of unsold newspapers to the car to be taken for disposal, Rebecca passed Jackie and her daughter,

Nicole, on the pavement. Warm greetings were exchanged among all three and Jackie and Nicole stepped into the shop.

As Rebecca drove Jean homewards towards Ashens Cottage they discussed an issue they had been pondering over for a while. Ashens was a few miles out of the village, right by the main road. The Pines had carried out a great deal of work on the house and it was comfortable, dry, warm and with all the needed facilities. They had also cleared an attractive garden space from the very substantial tract of land and forest adjacent to the house. While not spelling it out, the Pines had implicitly acknowledged to each other that they were not quite as young as they had once been. Recent chronic car troubles had emphasised the point that they should consider moving to a town where they would be close to shops, services and with easy access to the venues of their interests. It would mean selling Ashens Cottage and the shop as well, of course.

Rebecca and Jean's approach was to worry at such decisions leisurely, like a dog well fed and replete but slowly gnawing at a bone from time to time, in case the marrowbone jelly was the next gentle nibble away. They had found no conclusion when they reached Ashens Cottage and unpacking the car, Rebecca enquired after Jackie and whether she had called by for any special reason.

'No. She just popped in to see how we were both doing,' was the reply.

'That's good. They are both looking well, don't you think?' Rebecca smiled.

'Oh, and Kirsty was in the shop yesterday. I forgot to tell you. She has passed her exams as a dental nurse.'

'Jolly good. Well done, Kirsty.'

'Yes, they have all done well.'

~

Newman returned the telephone to its cradle. In her years of coming to Tarbert for weekends, she had disposed of almost everything about the Cottage, importing items more to her own particular taste. The telephone was an ancient, heavy, black object she had purchased in a specialist shop at considerable expense. Normally, she mocked the trend for buying pretend old with real new money but the telephone was of a different class and she abhorred the modern, plastic bleepers (available in ninety-eight colours, all garish). Newman spent a lot of time speaking on the telephone and the feel of that unforgiving device added gravitas to her spiel, or so she believed.

Looking around the room and once more at the loch, now sparkling in the low-slung sun, she picked up her case and left the Cottage.

~

Rebecca was sitting on her favourite chair enjoying hot, buttered crumpets Jean had prepared along with a steaming pot of tea. This was a room in which Rebecca felt comfortable and at ease and she cast her eye around, surveying the familiarity of it all. At the other side of the fireplace was her collection of Burns books. It had started with that first paperback edition when she was that young lad and had grown increasingly in importance as well as in number. She could choose any book off the shelf and open it with the intimacy of knowledge. Real books of a great poet. Around her were various objects, appearing as bric-a-brac to the unaccustomed eye but representing particular events and storing a raft of memories. Dusty, the cat, had sneaked up on the comfortable chair, under the bookshelf, and slept with the innocence of beasts and babes.

Lying on the coffee table was an old photograph album with images of a different time and different place, all carefully arranged and ordered. She had taken the collection downstairs when a visiting friend had asked her to tell him of her children. She had shown him pictures of Fiona and Duncan and told of the last time she had seen them and baby Alexander in a car park in Carlisle. How she feared she would not see them again. She had cried and cried at the memory, needing to stem the pain and the flow of tears with a poem written late that same night. Poetry helped her but could never replace the children she feared she had lost.

Across the room sat her Jean, sipping tea and reading a book, her beautiful, bright eyes squinting through the glass of her spectacles as she struggled to see the print in the failing light. Her Jean, whom she had almost lost twice but would never lose again. Her Jean, who had stood by her when others would have fled. Rebecca Pine knew that she was, indeed, a lucky woman.

A sweet-tasting melancholy had overcome Rebecca and she was grateful to the dimming of the day's light for concealing a tear, just one, which glazed her eye before sliding down a cheek.

All of her life, she had cried easily and freely. Fidgeting with the paper pad on her lap, she knew she would be unable to concentrate on her work just yet. To still her mood, Rebecca turned and stared out of the window behind her. A small window, in the original style of Ashens, it looked onto the main road, the darkness broken by the glare of passing car lamps. As the cars approached the cottage, their lights would rise, throwing a veil of white across the gable, through the panes and casting a silhouette of the woman's head onto the wall behind her.

~

Newman had stopped off in Tarbert, primarily to eat, but also to wander round some of the territory, touching landmarks all of which had grown to be of pervasive influence on her way of thinking of her life. Anger had been her companion for so long she had come to believe it was her rather than just part of her repertoire. She compared the changes she felt to that of a convert seeing the light, not so melodramatic but just as profound and twice as improbable. There was not one exact point in time when she could say she had changed. It was as if for ages she had been struggling to keep the ugly fury alive by aggravation and provocation. Years had been wasted and she needed help to stop blaming herself.

The daylight had almost gone by the time she climbed the steep path and walked tentatively past the houses, careful not to draw suspicious glances. Walking away from the domestic enclave, she encroached as close to the edge of the rocks as she dared. The land at the far side of the loch looked foreboding and fierce in the gloom. Newman took her time and looked at every angle and then at none as she closed her eyes, feeling the wind brush her face and rock her bodily to and fro.

Was this what Rebecca Pine was doing that day? Not needing to look, just feeling the air and being here? Was that enough for her?

~

Rebecca and Jean were sitting in their favourite room, restful and at peace with the evening and with each other. Jean had laid aside her book, the darkness finally drawing the blinds, and sat basking in the silence. Rebecca looked across at Jean and the two began speaking of their plans for the future, hoping the dark would bring enlightenment. The air in the room smelled of toasted crumpets, butter and books, and felt purposeful.

~

Newman was driving up the hill and out of Tarbert for the last time. In the boot of her car were two suitcases, one of clothes the other of books. Beside her on the passenger seat nestled the crow-like form of the telephone. She did not want anything else and had left the rest for whoever bought the Cottage. They would not find her difficult to deal with, being happy to have no lasting connection with the village. Her first act of grace would be to sell the Cottage to local people, a young family perhaps, at a cost without profit.

The departing Newman had one last homage to pay. She had debated with herself whether to somehow approach Rebecca and had planned various versions of what she would say. Nothing sounded right in rehearsal, being full of clichés or too obscure by far. How could Newman explain forty years of hate from a distance? Was it possible to explain to someone who does not know or remember you that you think them capable of great art, without seeming to be patronising or deranged? Or that she was born thirty years too soon? The conversation would not work and would not help Newman or Rebecca in any way.

Newman had abandoned all her prepared speeches, every last version, and had returned to an old theory of spontaneity. She would turn up at the door of Rebecca's home, knock and see what happened next.

Turning the sharp bend to the right, the one which warned her she was coming close to Ashens Cottage, Newman caught sight of a deer running across an adjacent field and up a green slope towards the horizon. Watching the hind sprint along and away from the road, free and easy, she felt her spirits rise, goading the deer to run faster and faster, to fly for us all but especially for Newman.

As her car climbed a slight incline and over a hump, she saw first a flash of the sign marking the entry for Stonefield Castle, then a twist to the left and the gable end of Ashens Cottage was illuminated. Anticipating the abrupt turn-off into Ashens' yard, Newman braked hard and came to an unscheduled halt, still on the main road. Sitting still, she dimmed the lights and watched the outline of Rebecca's head and shoulders by the cottage's window. Slowly, so slowly, Newman watched Rebecca staring sightless out of the window and straight at her before turning away and lowering her head.

The tree-lined road and black, low sky formed a tunnel in the beam of the headlamps, pulling Newman far away from Tarbert and Ashens and Rebecca for ever. Driving on, Newman whispered an oath of good fortune to her unknowing lifelong adversary-turned-mentor. 'Farewell and fortune for whatever you do and whoever you choose to be.'

~

Rebecca and Jean had just reached a decision. They would sell up the house and shop and buy another home in Tarbert, in the village where they would be close to everything and most of the people they needed. Tarbert had never been in any doubt, of course; the question was merely when and where, exactly. One day, perhaps, they would not be capable of the long drives to the cities to pursue their art and music. When that day arrived they both knew where they wanted to be marooned and where they wanted to stay.

Rebecca stared out of the window at the lights of a passing car and thanked the stars for her good fortune in finding Jean and both of them finding this place. The car sped past, onwards on its own journey and Rebecca turned back to the pad on her knee. Putting on a table lamp she picked up her pen, opened the manuscript and began to write.

My freedom is to be contained
within that person that I see is seen
in careless gaze of eyes unknown
that I should seem
to others than myself
no other than myself should be . . .

Index of Poems